Key Skills Level 2:
Communication

Written to the 2004 Standards

Roslyn Whitley Willis

Series Editor

Roslyn Whitley Willis

**Published by
Lexden Publishing Ltd
www.lexden-publishing.co.uk**

To ensure that your book is up to date visit:
www.lexden-publishing.co.uk/keyskills/update.htm

Acknowledgements

Thanks go to my husband for his contribution in naming some of the fictitious organisations that, and people who, appear in this book, together with his forbearance and encouragement.

I wish to say thank you to Mark for his invaluable contributions to this book and his continued dedication to the project.

I wish to dedicate this book to my father Peter Whitley – *Roslyn Whitley Willis*.

First Published in 2007 by Lexden Publishing Ltd.

Cover photograph of juggling balls by kind permission of Marcel Hol ©

British Library Cataloguing in Publication Data.

A CIP record of this book is available from the British Library.

ISBN: 978-1-904995-31-9

Typeset and designed by Lexden Publishing Ltd

Printed by Lightning Source.

Lexden Publishing Ltd
23 Irvine Road
Colchester
Essex CO3 3TS

Telephone: 01206 533164
Email: info@lexden-publishing.co.uk
www.lexden-publishing.co.uk

PREFACE

The material in this book gives you the opportunity to understand Key Skills and practise them so you are able to meet the high standards set out in the Level 2 Key Skills Standards for Communication.

The introductory section of this book explains each of the Key Skills and how to gain a qualification.

This book is further divided into three distinct parts:

1   Reference Sheets

This section provides all the necessary background information to prepare you for Level 2 Communication It provides useful exercises that will:

    aid your learning;

    can be used for revision; and

    prepare and aid you for the Part A Tasks and End Assessment questions.

2   Part A Practice Tasks

Working through these will help you produce work at the right level and prepare you for the End Assessment.

As you complete each task you will become more confident about what is expected in Key Skills and be able to use your knowledge and understanding to pass the End Assessment and put together a Portfolio of Evidence.

3   End Assessment Questions

This section provides examples of the type of questions that are likely to appear on an End Assessment paper and that you may have to pass as part of your Key Skills qualification.

Further resources

When your tutor thinks you have enough knowledge of Key Skills, she/he will give you an assignment, or assignments, to complete. Working successfully through the assignment(s) will show you are able to apply your knowledge and understanding, and produce work that will go into your Key Skills Portfolio of Evidence. These assignments are contained in the *Tutor's Resource* cd.

Additional resources and information can be found at www.lexden-publishing.co.uk/keyskills.

WHAT ARE KEY SKILLS? – A STUDENT'S GUIDE

Key Skills are important for everything you do, at school, at college, at work and at home. They will help you in your vocational studies and prepare you for the skills you will use in education and training and the work you will do in the future.

Key Skills are at the centre of your learning, and the work in this book provides you with the opportunity to develop and practise the Key Skills of Communication, Application of Number and Information and Communication Technology, through a variety of tasks. Having Key Skills knowledge will help you apply them to other areas of your studies.

There are six Key Skills

Communication is about writing and speaking.	**Application of Number** is about numbers.	**Information and Communication Technology** is about communicating using IT.
It will help you develop your skills in:	It will help you develop your skills in:	It will help you develop your skills in using computers to:
<ul><li>speaking;</li><li>listening;</li><li>researching;</li><li>reading;</li><li>writing;</li><li>presenting information in the form of text and images, including diagrams, charts and graphs.</li></ul>	<ul><li>collecting information;</li><li>carrying out calculations;</li><li>understanding the results of your calculations;</li><li>presenting your findings in a variety of ways, such as graphs and diagrams.</li></ul>	<ul><li>find and store information;</li><li>produce information using text and images and numbers;</li><li>develop your presentation of documents;</li><li>communicate information to other people.</li></ul>
Improving Own Learning and Performance is about planning and reviewing your work.	**Problem Solving** is about understanding and solving problems.	**Working with Others** is about working effectively with other people and giving support to them.
It will help you develop your skills in:	It will help you develop your skills in:	It will help you develop your skills in:
<ul><li>setting targets;</li><li>setting deadlines;</li><li>following your action plan of targets and deadlines;</li><li>reviewing your progress;</li><li>reviewing your achievements;</li><li>identifying your strengths and weaknesses.</li></ul>	<ul><li>identifying the problem;</li><li>coming up with solutions to the problem;</li><li>selecting ways of tackling the problem;</li><li>planning what you need to do to solve the problem;</li><li>following your plan;</li><li>deciding if you have solved the problem;</li><li>reviewing your problem solving techniques.</li></ul>	<ul><li>working with another, or several, person(s);</li><li>deciding on the roles and responsibilities of each person;</li><li>putting together an action plan of targets and responsibilities;</li><li>carrying out your responsibilities;</li><li>supporting other members of the group;</li><li>reviewing progress;</li><li>reviewing your achievements;</li><li>identifying the strengths and weaknesses of working with other people.</li></ul>

Mandatory Key Skills

Communication
Application of Number
ICT

Practise Part A Key
Skills tasks in this book
to help you:

Put together a
Portfolio of Evidence

Usually an assignment written for
you by your tutor to cover the Key
Skill, or a number of Key Skills in
one piece of work.

The Portfolio is based on Part B of
the Key Skill Standards.

Pass a test –
called an **End Assessment**

This test is 40 multiple-choice
questions and, at Levels 1 and 2,
you have either 1 hour or 1 hour 15
minutes to complete it depending on
the Key Skill.

The questions are based on Part A of
the Key Skill Standards.

Good News!

If you already have some GCSE or ICT
qualifications, it may not be necessary
for you to take the End Assessment! Your
tutor will help you with this – it is called
PROXY QUALIFICATIONS.

Wider Key Skills

Improving Own Learning and Performance
Problem Solving
Working with Others

Put together a **Portfolio of Evidence**

Usually included in an assignment written for you by
your tutor to cover the Key Skills of Communication,
Application of Number or ICT.

The Portfolio is based on Part B of the Key Skill
Standards.

Practise Part A Key Skills
tasks in your vocational
studies to help you:

Opportunities to work towards achieving the Wider Key Skills are provided in the Portfolio assignment work and
are included in the *Tutor's Resource* that accompanies this text.

THE PORTFOLIO

STEP 1

Once your tutor has assessed your assignment work and you have passed, you will put your work into your portfolio.

A **Portfolio of Evidence** usually takes the form of a lever arch file with a **Portfolio Front Sheet** that shows:

 where you are studying;

 which course you are studying;

 which Key Skill(s) are in the portfolio;

 when you passed your End Assessment(s); and

 details of any Proxy Qualifications.

STEP 2

It is important to number every page of the work you put in your portfolio. This helps you complete the **Log Book** that your tutor will give you.

STEP 3

Complete the Log Book. This indicates where your evidence is to be found and also describes what is in the portfolio.

STEP 4

Check your Log Book entries carefully, making sure everything is correct and neat.

Get your tutor to check you have put your Portfolio together correctly.

STEP 5

Sign the Log Book and get the person who assessed your work to sign too.

Once you have completed your Portfolio of Evidence it is shown to someone outside your centre whose job it is to check it meets the Key Skills Standards. If this person agrees that it does, then you have **passed your Portfolio of Evidence**.

Communication

At **Level 2**, learners need to use the skills of speaking, listening, reading and writing. You will be able to take part in discussions using a varied vocabulary and help to move the discussion forward so that it flows freely and allows everyone to contribute.

Learners will be able to select reading material from a variety of sources. Such material will contain up to 500 words and will be on a variety of topics . You will show you can summarise this material, correctly following the meaning of the documents. You will be able to write documents, some of them up to 500 words in length, to suit the purpose of the task, and the audience who will read it. You will include relevant images in some of the documents you write. Your work will be correctly spelt and punctuated and you will use correct grammar. Learners will give a short talk that will last at least four minutes.

The following Reference Sheets provide opportunities for you to review and practise the Communication skills needed for Key Skills.

Writing and setting out memos — 6
A memorandum — 6
Informal memo — 7
Taking messages — 8
Identifying the key facts — 8
Using images in communication — 10
Presenting numerical data in visual form — 10
Advertisements — 12
Line advertisements — 12
Display advertisements — 12
Column advertisements (in newspapers and magazines) — 13
Designing advertisements — 13
Writing and setting out business letters — 14
Introductory paragraph — 14
Middle paragraph(s) — 14
Closing paragraph — 14
Useful phrases for business letters — 16
Using the telephone and making telephone calls — 17
Before you place a call — 17
How to speak on the telephone — 17
Making telephone calls — 17
How to answer a ringing telephone — 17
Good manners on the telephone — 17
Writing and setting out personal letters — 18
Some points to remember about letter writing — 18

Examples of address, salutation and complimentary close — 19
A personal letter written to a company — 20
An informal personal letter to a friend — 21
Writing reports — 22
Points to consider before beginning your report — 22
Structuring a report — 23
Parts of a report — 23
The report's content — 25
Writing a bibliography — 26
Giving a talk or presentation — 27
The five main stages in preparing for a talk or presentation — 27
Delivering your presentation — 27
Images — 28
Never read it out! — 28
Creating an opener — 28
What openers can you use? — 28
Closing with a flourish — 28
It's question time! – Handling questions — 28
Commonly misspelt words — 29
Communication: Part A, Practice Tasks — 35
Sample End Assessment — 63
Index — 68

WRITING AND SETTING OUT MEMOS

A memorandum – plural memoranda
(abbreviated to memo)

A memo is an **internal** method of communication.

Memos must be short documents, and usually deal with one subject. A long document within an organisation is usually sent in the form of a report.

The memo should be signed by the sender.

Although organisations have their own style of layout for memos, all memos contain these essential headings:

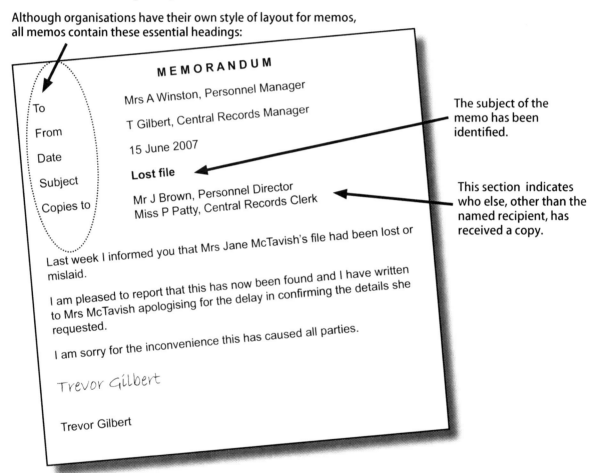

MEMORANDUM

Mrs A Winston, Personnel Manager

T Gilbert, Central Records Manager

15 June 2007

Lost file

Mr J Brown, Personnel Director
Miss P Patty, Central Records Clerk

To
From
Date
Subject
Copies to

The subject of the memo has been identified.

This section indicates who else, other than the named recipient, has received a copy.

Last week I informed you that Mrs Jane McTavish's file had been lost or mislaid.

I am pleased to report that this has now been found and I have written to Mrs McTavish apologising for the delay in confirming the details she requested.

I am sorry for the inconvenience this has caused all parties.

Trevor Gilbert

Trevor Gilbert

Typical layout of a memorandum (memo). This is formal as it includes their titles (Mr, Mrs, Personnel Manager, etc.).

In this example you will see the message is short and simple and deals with only one point.

Who the memo is from, and to whom it is being sent, are identified and the document is dated and signed.

Informal memo

This is an example of an **informal** memo:

MEMORANDUM

To — Janet Markham, Advertising Department

From — Catherine Woodleigh, Purchasing Department

Date — 15 June 2007

Re — Company's Sales Brochure

The 2,000 copies of the company's Christmas brochure have been received from the printer today.

These are available for you to collect at your earliest convenience.

Catherine

In this example, the names have no title and there are no job titles included – although people's departments are shown. This is important because an organisation could employ people with the same name but who work in different departments.

The memo is dated. There is a subject – this time expressed as 're' (short for 'reference').

The memo is signed with the sender's first name only – the surname could be included.

TAKING MESSAGES

It is always helpful to use a standard message form to record a message, whether it is a telephone message or a message of another kind. The headings on a standard form will help you include the information needed.

There is a message form on *page 9*, but this is not the only layout that companies use.

Remember you should always:

 Use simple, straightforward words.

 Keep your sentences short but vary the length a little so that the message reads well.

 Include **all, and only, the key facts and information.**

 Leave out irrelevant information.

 If you are repeating a request for the reader of the message to **do something**, make it a request **not an order**.

 Be very specific and clear about days, dates and times. If you have to give a non-specific time, e.g. "tomorrow", add the day and date in case your message is not read immediately. It is advisable to always be specific about days and dates in order to avoid confusion.

 Mark urgent messages clearly.

Your responsibility does not end when you place the message on the right desk – it only ends when the person has read it and understood it.

Identifying the key facts

Every message contains key facts. If you miss them out of the message it will not make sense – or not make **complete sense**.

Business callers are normally quite good at giving the key facts in an ordered way and checking them through afterwards. Private callers may be less helpful and some may like to chat, so that it becomes difficult to sort out what is important from what is not.

A good way to check you have the message clear in your mind is to read back your summary to the caller. This both checks that you have the message correctly with all the important facts, and gives the caller the opportunity to alter or add anything.

> **Note**
>
> This page includes the word **message**. This is a commonly misspelt word that you should be familiar with and learn to spell correctly. We have provided a document of commonly misspelt words that can be downloaded at www.lexden-publishing.co.uk/keyskills or ask your tutor for a copy. Use this to learn the words that cause you problems.

MESSAGE FORM

TO...DEPARTMENT...

DATE ....TIME ....

CALLER'S NAME...

ORGANISATION ....

TELEPHONE NUMBER...FAX NUMBER...

EMAIL ADDRESS ....

✓ Appropriate box(es)

Telephoned	☐
Returned your call	☐
Called to see you	☐
Left a message	☐
Requests you call back	☐
Please arrange an appointment	☐

Message

....

....

....

....

....

....

....

Taken by .... Department.. Time..........................

USING IMAGES IN COMMUNICATION

Images can be used to enhance and explain written communications.

Remember, use images to **enhance the text**, and to help the reader's understanding of the text. An image may also provide information in addition to text. **An image should not be included if it has no relevance**.

Think carefully about why you are using images and only use appropriate images in appropriate places.

Presenting numerical data in visual form

There are a number of situations when you will find it necessary, or preferable, to produce visual representations of numbers. Some people find it easier to understand figures when presented in graphical form, rather than table form. By all means consider using both a table and a graph, thus providing a number of ways in which the reader can understand the information.

Data in tabular form

INTERNATIONAL TEMPERATURES		
3rd January 2006		
CITY	MIN	MAX
Lisbon	10	14
Madrid	-2	12
London	3	12
Brussels	6	10
Amsterdam	6	8
Helsinki	1	2

Data in graphical form

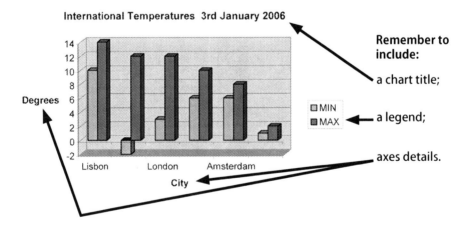

Remember to include:
- a chart title;
- a legend;
- axes details.

The purpose of including the chart and the table is to allow the reader to understand and interpret the information in the most suitable way.

10

CRUISING ON THE AIDAblu
– a P&O* Cruise Liner

Imagine... it's 7.30 am and the sun is just beginning to rise above the mountains that run down to the sea... you've had breakfast in one of the four restaurants... you are on deck watching the beautiful island of Madeira get closer as your floating, luxury hotel edges slowly into port... the forecast for the day ahead is 28°... you've all day to explore today's destination and will probably have dinner in one of the restaurants as AIDAblu leaves port at 8 pm.

Come and experience the relaxing life on board our latest cruise liner

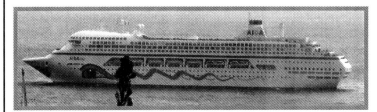

The AIDAblu entering the port of Funchal, Madeira

We'll include visits to some of the most beautiful islands and ports in the Atlantic

*A member of Dubai Ports World

The inclusion of an image in this article helps the reader to identify the 'product' that is being discussed and adds interest to facts and figures.

In this instance, the *text* is being used to aid the readers' understanding of the images.

WEATHER UK
20th February 2006

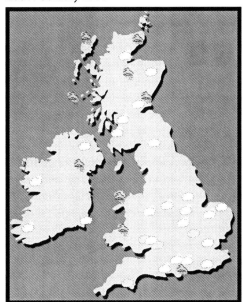

**WEATHER UK
20th February 2006**

Norfolk and Suffolk

There are few clouds at 2000 feet

Visibility is 7000m

Cornwall and Devon

Light rain at 1300 feet

Broken rain clouds at 1600 feet

Wind speed 18-36 mph

ADVERTISEMENTS

Advertisements may be placed in newspapers or magazines for a number of reasons, including:

 to advertise jobs;

 to promote products or services;

 to announce special events or functions;

 to publicise changes in an organisation;

 to recall faulty goods.

The **Classified Advertisements** section of a newspaper allows quick reference to a wide range of advertisements which are usually inserted according to subject.

Line advertisements

> GOOD BUY, BRAND new telephone/fax/copier/scanner for sale. Owner is relocating abroad. Tel: 0184 576399

This information runs from line-to-line, often using the same typeface throughout, with no special layout. Charges are made by the line, normally with a minimum charge for three or four lines.

In such advertisements (also know as lineage ads), an opening should be made which catches the readers' attention, and then as much abbreviated information as possible should be contained in as few lines as possible.

Display advertisements

These may use a variety of fonts and sizes, and may be illustrated with artwork and colour. Charges are based on the number of column centimetres, often with a minimum size. Information can be displayed within the advertisement to attract attention to special features.

Column advertisements (in newspapers and magazines)

The pages of newspapers and magazines are divided into **columns** and advertisers purchase so many column widths. The publisher charges so much per column and depth of advertisement.

In this example the page has been divided into four columns. Hop, Skip and Jump has taken an advertisement over two columns.

HOP, SKIP AND JUMP

Shoe manufacturers of quality

END OF SEASON SALE

Leather Uppers ● Leather Soles
● Luxury Comfort Linings

Sizes 5, 6, 7, 8, 9, 10 and 11.

Brogue	Black	Brogue	Brown
Oxford	Black	Oxford	Brown
Casual	Black	Casual	Brown
Lace	Black	Lace	Brown

Telephone to place an order TODAY

Whilst stocks last

0165 7873 9882

Designing advertisements

Designing an advertisement is an exercise in **summarising**. It is important to pick out the main points, features, advantages, or whatever is relevant to the theme of the advertisement.

It is essential to ensure the advertisement will be **seen** on the page of the newspaper or magazine. If it is displayed unattractively, it will not achieve this objective. Here are some guidelines:

- Use a company logo, prominently displayed. People can identify with a well-known logo.

- Whatever is being advertised, display the headline **PROMINENTLY** using bold text, underlining, **ALL CAPITALS**, for instance.

- Break up the information sensibly and logically; perhaps various points could be listed using an asterisk or a bullet point.

- Use spacing and balance sensibly – remember the more space you use the more you will pay!

- Try to achieve a progressive display which categorises information logically, leading finally to action required by the reader – "visit us on ???" "Contact us", etc.

WRITING AND SETTING OUT BUSINESS LETTERS

A business letter is an **external** method of communication and reflects how an organisation communicates with, and is viewed by, people and organisations outside the business.

There are a number of purposes for business letters:

 providing information;

 giving instructions;

 confirming arrangements;

 improving customer services;

 public relations.

A business letter has three parts:

1 introductory paragraph;

2 middle paragraph(s);

3 closing paragraph.

Introductory paragraph

The introduction/opening paragraph introduces the theme/purpose of the letter and puts it into a context or provides a background.

Introductory paragraphs are also used to mention essential people, events or things to which the letter will refer.

Middle paragraph(s)

These provide detailed information.

The middle paragraphs of a letter **develop a theme** and **provide all relevant details** and particulars. The number of paragraphs used will depend upon the complexity of the letter's subject. However, paragraphs should be kept fairly short and deal with only one topic at a time. **New topic = new paragraph** is something you must keep in mind.

Closing paragraph

This provides an action statement and a courteous close.

In this paragraph you will attempt to summarise your comments and state what action you will take, or wish to be taken.

Some letters are concluded with a courteous sentence to act as a means of signalling the end of the document.

WITH CARE
AIR CARGO HANDLING PLC

Hanger 18R, Manchester Airport, Manchester MR4 6JE
0161 346 98667
email: **withcare@manair.aviation.com**

A

B

23 March 2006

Mr Peter Phillips
Despatch Department Manager
Mercury Components plc
Unit 7
Coniston Industrial Park
BARNSLEY
South Yorkshire
SO13 6BN

C

Dear Mr Phillips

D

E

AIR FREIGHT TO CHICAGO 4 April 2007

F

Thank you for your company's recent request to quote for transporting a packing crate to Chicago.

As you know, our Mike Richards came to your organisation yesterday to examine the crate, take its measurements and establish its weight. As a result of his visit we are pleased to be able to quote the sum of £568.90 + VAT. Our formal quotation is enclosed with this letter.

For this sum we will:

- collect the crate on 2 April before 12 noon

G

- transport it to our depot at Manchester Airport

- ensure the paperwork for its journey is in order

- obtain UK Customs clearance for the crate

- put it on flight WC457 departing at 15:20 hours on 4 April, for Chicago O'Hare Airport

- upon arrival, arrange for our American handlers to unload the crate and obtain US Customs clearance

- store safely in the depot until your US client collects the crate.

We trust this quotation is acceptable and look forward to assisting you on this occasion. We would need confirmation of your wish to employ our services no later than 28 March.

If you wish to discuss this matter further, please do not hesitate to contact me.

H

My direct line number is 0161 346 2323.

Yours sincerely

I

Paul Falcon
Procurement Manager
Enc

J

Key to parts of a business letter

(A) The **letter heading** of the company including a company logo.

(B) **Date** expressed as dd/mm/yyyy.

(C) **Name**, **title** and **company name** and **address** of the person and company receiving the letter.

(D) **Salutation** – Dear Mr Phillips because the letter is addressed to him in the name and address line.

(E) **Heading**: indicating what the letter is about.

(F) **Introductory paragraph**.

(G) **Middle paragraphs** providing details.

(H) **Closing paragraphs** providing an action statement and a courteous close.

(I) **Complimentary close**: Yours sincerely because the recipient's name is used in the salutation. The writer's name and title, leaving space for his signature!

(J) **Enc** indicating there is an enclosure.

Useful phrases for business letters

Thank you for your letter dated ....

As you may know ....

I wish to inform you that ....

I was pleased to hear that ....

I wish to enquire about ....

I should like to place an order for ....

I look forward to hearing from you in the near future.

I should be grateful if you would kindly send me ....

Following our recent telephone conversation, I wish to ....

Please do not hesitate to let me know if I can do anything further to help ....

USING THE TELEPHONE AND MAKING TELEPHONE CALLS

Before you place a call

- Think about what you wish to say and how you will say it. Courtesy is expected when using the telephone just as if you are talking in person.

- Make a list of what you need to say and the information you need to give and/or receive **before placing the call**. **BE PREPARED**.

- Dialling too quickly may be the cause of dialling a wrong number, never just hang up. Apologise and let the person who answered the telephone know you have dialled the incorrect number.

How to speak on the telephone

- When speaking, think of the way you sound. On the telephone sounds and moods are magnified. **Talk with a smile in your voice**. The person on the other end of the telephone cannot see your facial expressions and your tone of voice will need to express politeness, enthusiasm and efficiency.

- Make sure you say your words clearly and precisely. It is embarrassing, and time-wasting, to be asked to repeat what you are saying. Names and addresses are particularly difficult, so say yours slowly, spelling any unusual words.

Making telephone calls

- It is polite, and necessary, to identify yourself. If you are calling from a company, then you would need to identify your company, your name, and perhaps your department, before going on to say why you are calling. For instance:

  Good morning, this is Blackwood and Company of York. Janet speaking from the Purchasing Department. I am ringing to place an order...... I wish to speak to ....

How to answer a ringing telephone

- The proper way to answer the telephone is give a greeting – **hello; good afternoon** – followed by identifying your telephone number if it is your home, or your name and your company. **Never** answer with just "hello" or "yes". Hello is useless because it does not tell the caller anything, and "yes" is curt and impolite, and again it does not tell the caller anything – except perhaps that you are in a bad mood and cannot be bothered.

Good manners on the telephone

- Answer a ringing telephone promptly.

- If you dial a number that is wrong, apologise promptly and hang up.

- Calling a business at or very near closing time is thoughtless and not likely to result in a successful call.

- Introduce yourself when placing a call.

- Answer a phone by identifying yourself, your company and/or your department.

- When speaking to anyone who is working and for whom time is important, make your call informative and short – plan ahead.

- It is polite to let the person who **made** the call **end** the call.

WRITING AND SETTING OUT PERSONAL LETTERS

A personal letter is a letter written from someone's home address to either:

 a company – for instance to accompany a job application, or to complain about something; or

 a friend – for instance to invite a friend to stay with you.

Some points to remember about letter writing

 Firstly: the date.

Put the date the letter is written. This date should be shown as:

dd/mm/yyyy

that is: 14th June 2005. Do not mix this order.

 Secondly: the name and address to where the letter is being sent.

Remember to write to a **person** if you can;

that is: Mr Jaz Allahan.

If you don't know the name of the person, address the letter to a job title;

that is: The Marketing Manager.

> *If it is an informal letter to a friend, it is acceptable to omit the name and address.*

> **Remember**
>
> Don't just write Allahan and Corby Ltd. A COMPANY cannot open a letter, but a PERSON can!

 Thirdly: who are you writing to?

When you write "Dear ...." it is called the **salutation**.

When you write "Yours ...." it is called the **complimentary close**.

The salutation and complimentary close must match.

That is: Dear Mr Jones = Yours sincerely

Dear Sirs = Yours faithfully

When you use a person's name, be sincere!

> *In an informal letter to a friend you can write "Dear Patrick".*

> *If it is an informal letter to a friend you just need to write "Best wishes" or "Kind regards" and sign your first name.*

> **Note**
>
> Only the word *Yours* has a capital letter at the beginning.

 Fourthly: sign the letter.

A letter from you needs to be signed. After the complimentary close, leave yourself space for a signature, then print your name. This is important because your signature may not be readable and the person who receives the letter will not know your name.

Examples of address, salutation and complimentary close

Name and address:	Mr P Marks Sunningbrow Golf Course Sunningbrow Hill Aberdeen AB7 3NH
Salutation:	Dear Mr Marks
	Never write Dear Mr P Marks – just Dear Mr Marks. Think of how you would address him if meeting him. You would say "Mr Marks", so write it as you would say it.
Complimentary close:	Yours sincerely
	You have used his name, so be SINCERE!

Name and address:	The Sales Manager McKie and Aston plc 8 School Fields York YO14 5ND
Salutation:	Dear Sir or Madam
	because you have not used a name
Complimentary close:	Yours faithfully
	You have not used a name, so how can you be SINCERE!

Name and address:	Mrs K Trent Office Manager T&N Agency Villamoura Road Bexhill on Sea Sussex SX5 7BQ	**This time you have used a name and a job title.**
Salutation:	Dear Mrs Trent	
	because you have addressed the letter to her	
Complimentary close:	Yours sincerely	
	You have used her name, so be SINCERE!	

A personal letter written to a company

The following is an example of a personal letter written to a company:

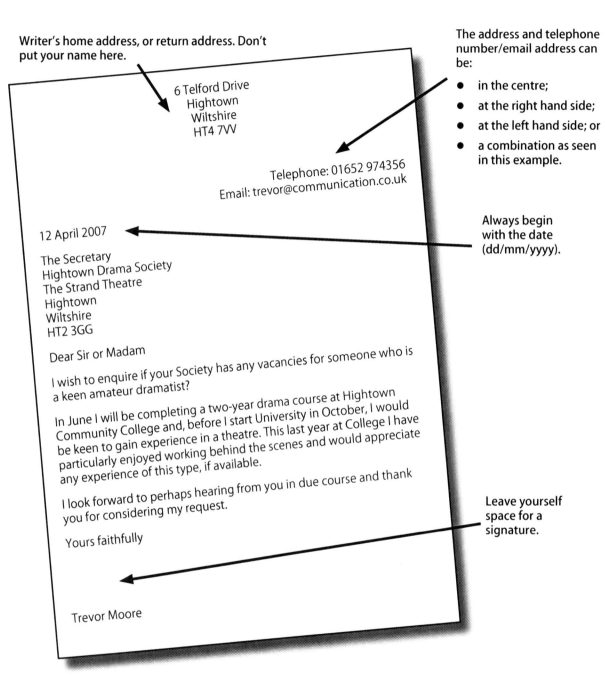

Writer's home address, or return address. Don't put your name here.

6 Telford Drive
Hightown
Wiltshire
HT4 7VV

Telephone: 01652 974356
Email: trevor@communication.co.uk

12 April 2007

The Secretary
Hightown Drama Society
The Strand Theatre
Hightown
Wiltshire
HT2 3GG

Dear Sir or Madam

I wish to enquire if your Society has any vacancies for someone who is a keen amateur dramatist?

In June I will be completing a two-year drama course at Hightown Community College and, before I start University in October, I would be keen to gain experience in a theatre. This last year at College I have particularly enjoyed working behind the scenes and would appreciate any experience of this type, if available.

I look forward to perhaps hearing from you in due course and thank you for considering my request.

Yours faithfully

Trevor Moore

The address and telephone number/email address can be:

- in the centre;
- at the right hand side;
- at the left hand side; or
- a combination as seen in this example.

Always begin with the date (dd/mm/yyyy).

Leave yourself space for a signature.

An informal personal letter to a friend

The following is an example of an informal personal letter written to a friend:

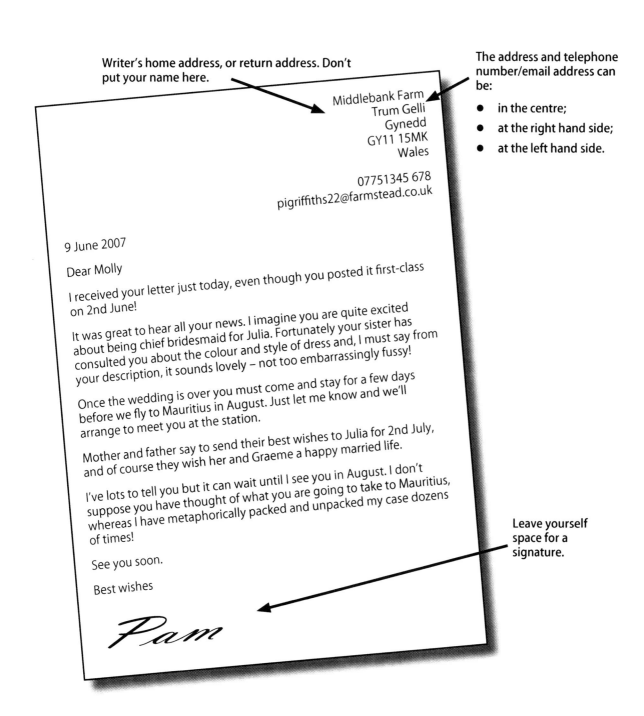

Writer's home address, or return address. Don't put your name here.

The address and telephone number/email address can be:

- in the centre;
- at the right hand side;
- at the left hand side.

Middlebank Farm
Trum Gelli
Gynedd
GY11 15MK
Wales

07751345 678
pigriffiths22@farmstead.co.uk

9 June 2007

Dear Molly

I received your letter just today, even though you posted it first-class on 2nd June!

It was great to hear all your news. I imagine you are quite excited about being chief bridesmaid for Julia. Fortunately your sister has consulted you about the colour and style of dress and, I must say from your description, it sounds lovely – not too embarrassingly fussy!

Once the wedding is over you must come and stay for a few days before we fly to Mauritius in August. Just let me know and we'll arrange to meet you at the station.

Mother and father say to send their best wishes to Julia for 2nd July, and of course they wish her and Graeme a happy married life.

I've lots to tell you but it can wait until I see you in August. I don't suppose you have thought of what you are going to take to Mauritius, whereas I have metaphorically packed and unpacked my case dozens of times!

See you soon.

Best wishes

Pam

Leave yourself space for a signature.

WRITING REPORTS

In common with any other business document, a report needs to be planned and, before beginning, you must consider the following:

 A report will usually be requested by people who need the information for a specific purpose.

 A report differs from an essay in that it is designed to provide information that will be acted on, rather than to be read by people interested in the ideas for their own sake. Because of this, it has a different structure and layout.

 Do not write in the first person.

 Use the past tense to describe your findings.

"It was found that......... etc., etc". **It** rather than **I** and the past tense of the verb to find, i.e. **found**.

Points to consider before beginning your report

For whom am I writing the report?

 A named individual, or a group of people?

 Person(s) who have no knowledge of the subject matter?

 What do the readers need to know?

 What do the readers already know?

What is my objective?

 To inform the readers?

 To explain ideas?

 To persuade?

 To consult?

 To transmit ideas or information, facts or findings?

 To make recommendations about ways of doing things, making improvements or changes?

What is the context?

 Urgent/important?

 Routine or "one-off"?

 Stand alone, or linked with a presentation?

 Sensitive?

What source material?

Is it readily available?

Do I need to do any research?

If you skip the planning stage, poor preparation invariably causes time-consuming problems at a later stage.

Structuring a report

A report is used for reference and is often quite a lengthy document. It has to be clearly structured for you and your readers to quickly find the information it contains.

Parts of a report

The nature of the report will vary from routine reports to complex, non-routine reports. The layout will vary too, yet all reports should have the following common features:

Cover sheet

This should contain the following:

 full title of the report;

 your name;

 the name of the person(s) for whom the report is intended;

 the date.

Terms of reference

This refers to:

 the main subject of the report;

 the scope and purpose of the report;

 the audience who will read it.

The terms of reference should tell you:

 what the report is going to discuss;

 why it is being produced;

 who will read it.

You need to know this information before you begin the process of producing the report:

what? + why? + who? = terms of reference

Title

When you have established the Terms of Reference you can consider the Title.

For any title to be of value it must:

 reflect the terms of reference;

 be precise and refer directly to the subject of the report.

Main sections/findings

The report will need to be divided into various logical sections and sub-sections. Make full use of **paragraph headings** and **paragraph numbering** including **bullet points**.

This is the section in which you:

 state what you found out;

 clearly present your results, making use of paragraphs, paragraph headings, bullet points, etc.;

 list the essential data. You may want to use tables, graphs and figures.

Use a consistent system of display throughout. Numbered paragraphs might be 1, 2, 3, or 1.1, 1.2, 1.3, etc.

Using effective "signposting" in this way will help the reader pick out elements of the report and will ensure the whole document is easy to follow.

Conclusions

Remember, the purpose of a report is to provide findings and draw conclusions from those findings. This section is vital in a report and allows the key arguments and findings of the report to be drawn together and put into context.

Conclusions need to:

 refer to the purpose of the report;

 state the main points arising in the report;

 be brief and concise.

Recommendations

Any recommendations you make must be presented clearly and follow logically from the conclusions.

This section might, for example, suggest a preferred option from several that were under consideration, make new proposals or recommend further research or investigation.

Bibliography

List all the sources that you have referred to in the main sections of the report. (*See page 26 on Writing a bibliography.*)

A sample title page of a report

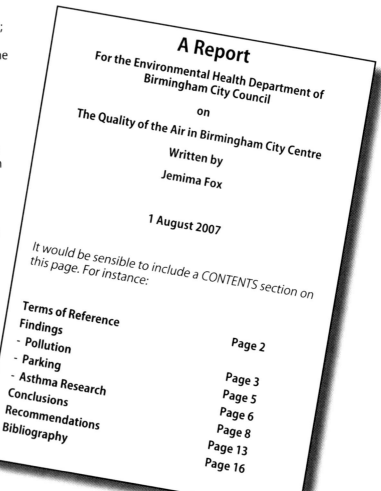

A Report

For the Environmental Health Department of Birmingham City Council

on

The Quality of the Air in Birmingham City Centre

Written by

Jemima Fox

1 August 2007

It would be sensible to include a CONTENTS section on this page. For instance:

Terms of Reference
Findings
- Pollution   Page 2
- Parking
- Asthma Research   Page 3
Conclusions   Page 5
Recommendations   Page 6
Bibliography   Page 8
    Page 13
    Page 16

The report's content

Terms of reference

Report on "The Quality of the Air in Birmingham City Centre" for the Environmental Health Department of the City Council, in order that it can consider possible traffic limiting proposals in the City Centre during peak weekday periods.

Title

The Quality of the Air in Birmingham City Centre

Findings

This report was requested by   (*person(s)*) in order that   (*what the persons are going to do with the report findings*).

In order to produce this report it was necessary to conduct research into the following topics:

....

....

....

and the sources consulted are listed separately in the Bibliography on page X.

1   Pollution.

         Make an opening statement about the topic and its relevance to the report then separate into sub-headings, which may, or may not, be numbered.

1.1   UK city average pollution figures.

1.2   City pollution figures related to increase in the number of Asthma sufferers.

1.3   etc., etc., etc.

2   Parking.

Conclusions

The purpose of this Report was to .... As can be understood from the information contained in "Findings", there is overwhelming evidence that the City of Birmingham's City Centre has the second highest pollution figures in the UK................. etc., etc., etc.

Go on to summarise your findings.

Recommendations

The Environmental Health Committee will consider the content of this report when deciding whether to limit traffic in the City Centre during peak periods of the week.

In view of the evidence, the recommendations to the Committee are as follows:

Describe the recommendations, making use of paragraphs, paragraph headings, bullet points, underlined headings, emboldened text, etc.

A report is a business document so you must sign it at the end.

Bibliography

List the documents you consulted in your research here.

Writing a bibliography

A **bibliography** is a list of sources you have consulted and used information from, for such documents as a report, essay or presentation.

The bibliography is usually produced as an **Appendix** and the information is displayed in categories (books, reference books, newspaper articles, web sites). Each **category heading** appears in alphabetical order and under each **category heading**, the sources are arranged alphabetically. (*See Example 1 below.*)

Example 1

Bibliography

Books

Anderson, M, 2005, *The history of needlework*, Swan & Signet Books, Preston.

Connaught, J P, 2001, *British needlework explained*, Mercantile Books, Edinburgh.

Newspaper Articles

Silvester, C, 2003, 'UK needlework trends since 1851', *The Nottingham Gazette*, 7 April 2003, p15.

Uxbridge, K, 2004, 'Needles and Threads', *The Cornish Messenger*, 20 September 2004, pp49 and 50.

Reference Books

The Encyclopedia of European Embroidery, 2002, 3rd edition, Stitch-in-Time Publishing, Worcester.

Threads Galore, 2005, 1st edition, Sharp Publishing, Norwich.

Web Sites

Ruby, J T 2006, The UK Needlework Association, Nottingham, viewed 24 August 2006 www.uk-nan.org.uk.

Westward, H and Prentice, B 2005, Simply Needlework, Colchester, viewed 25 August 2006

www.simplyneedlework.com.

There is a recommended **list** of information that should be included in each category, and a recommended **order** in which this information should be presented. Some of this information is separated by a comma and some appears in *italics*.

Books	Newspaper articles
Author's name, comma, initial(s), comma	Author's name, comma
Date of publication, comma	Initial(s), comma
Title in italics, comma	Date, comma
Publisher, comma	Title of article in **single quotations (')**, comma
City/town of publication (not country), full stop.	*Title of newspaper* in italics, comma
	Date of publication, comma
	Page number(s) of the article, full stop.
Reference books	**Web sites**
Title of book in italics, comma	Author (person or organisation), comma
Year, comma	Date (site created or updated), comma
Edition, comma	Name of publisher, comma
Publisher, comma	City of the publisher, comma
City of publication full stop.	Date you viewed the site
	URL, full stop.

GIVING A TALK OR PRESENTATION

The ability to make an oral presentation is an important skill. In today's workplace employees will be required to address colleagues, or external groups, from time to time, and it is also increasingly common for some job interviews to include an oral presentation.

The five main stages in preparing for a talk or presentation

STAGE 1

Address and answer the main questions related to the topic, i.e. **be clear about the purpose of the talk or presentation**.

STAGE 2

Be clear about your brief, i.e. **work out exactly who is your audience, what they know about the topic already (if anything), and what you intend them to know afterwards**.

STAGE 3

Decide what to include, and what **not** to include.

STAGE 4

Decide how to organise the material.

STAGE 5

Make the structure and sequence **logical**.

> **"Your brain starts working from the moment you are born and never stops, until you stand up to speak in public."** *Sir George Jessel*

> **THOROUGH PREPARATION IS VITAL TO SUCCESS**

Delivering your presentation

- It is preferable to stand when you are speaking unless it is an informal presentation to a small group.

- Ask your audience if they can see and hear you and any material you may be using (overhead projector slides (OHPs), whiteboards, flipcharts, etc.)

- Try to use your OHPs or software slides as a prompt so that you do not have to use notes.

- If you do not feel confident enough to do this, then notes on cards are easy to hold. If you use word-processed notes, use a typeface that you can read easily and a type size of 14 point or more and space them out so that they are easy to see at a glance. **Highlighting** key words helps.

- Do not use technical jargon without being prepared to explain it to your audience. Do not assume your audience is as familiar with your topic as you are.

- Do not speak too fast. Vary your pace and, if your voice is normally quiet, then speak a little louder than usual.

- Keep eye contact with your audience. Include the people on the edges of the group. Eye contact keeps your audience engaged in your presentation. Do not address the projector screen!

- Do not fiddle with pens, pointers, etc. when speaking. Do not jangle keys or cash in your pocket. Try to keep still.

- If you are one member of a group making a presentation decide how you are going to divide the presentation up? Who is going to do what?

Images

Amongst other things, images serve to:

 add interest to what you are saying;

 focus the audience's attention;

 clarify facts;

 help the audience remember what you say.

Never read it out!

Nervous speakers often make the mistake of reading from their script. This tactic results in a head down, zero eye-contact, monotonous lecture, not an interesting talk with the speaker engaging the audience's attention and interest.

Of course, you know your topic well, having prepared it well, so now prepare a series of **cues** in the form of notes on cards to prompt you about your topic. Your talk will be based on these cues, not on a script!

Creating an opener

At the beginning tell the audience the context of your talk and a brief outline of what you are going to cover.

How do you first secure the attention of the audience?

They will want to know two things:

 that your message is relevant and interesting to them; and

 that you have the presence/credibility necessary to deliver it.

What openers can you use?

Ask a relevant question "Let me begin by asking you a question …………"

Quote a statistic "Did you know that X% of people in the UK …………"

Use a relevant quotation

Follow these up with a brief explanation of **who you are** and **what you are going to talk about**, emphasising what members of the audience will gain by listening.

Closing with a flourish

The close is the equivalent to the conclusion section of a report or a letter – where you draw arguments and facts together.

Remind everyone of the objectives of the talk/presentation, and summarise your key points.

"So before I finish, I'd like to summarise the points we've covered this afternoon …………"

It's question time! – Handling questions

 Allow time at the end of your presentation for questions.

 Tell your audience at the beginning when you want to receive questions, to avoid interruptions. For short, time-limited presentations it is best to leave questions to the end. Otherwise you may not have time to finish your presentation.

COMMONLY MISSPELT WORDS

Word	word with different ending(s)	Word	word with different ending(s)
A		**B**	
A lot		Bachelor	
Absence	Absent	Balloon	Ballooning
Accommodate	Accommodation	Beauty	Beautiful
Achieve	Achievement	Begin	Beginner
Acknowledge		Believe	Believing
Acknowledgement		Benefit	Benefited
	Acknowledging		Benefiting
Acquire	Acquiring	Burglar	Burglary
Across		Business	
Address	Addresses		
	Addressing	**C**	
Advertise	Advertising		
	Advertisement	Calendar	
Agree	Agreement	Careful	Carefully
	Agreeable	Carriage	
All right		Category	Categories
Already		Chief	Chiefly
Altogether		Circuit	
Amount	Amounted	Colleague	
	Amounting	College	
Analyse	Analysis	Commemorate	Commemoration
	Analysing	Commission	Commissioner
Apparent	Apparently	Compare	Comparison
Appear	Appearing		Comparatively
	Appearance	Competent	Competently
Appropriate	Appropriately	Complete	Completely
Argue	Argument	Condemn	Condemning
	Arguing		Condemnation
Article			Condemnatory
Associate	Association	Conscience	
Attach	Attached	Consistent	Consistently
	Attachment	Courteous	Courteously
Attitude		Curious	Curiously
Author			Curiosity
Awkward	Awkwardly		
	Awkwardness		

Word	word with different ending(s)
D	
Daughter	
Decent	Decently
Decide	Decision
Defend	Defence
Definite	Definition
Democracy	
Descend	Descending
	Descendant
Despair	
Desperate	Desperately
	Desperation
Detached	
Deter	Deterrent
	Deterring
Deteriorate	Deterioration
Develop	Developing
	Development
Different	Differently
	Difference
Dilemma	
Disappear	Disappearance
	Disappearing
Disaster	Disastrous
Discipline	Disciplining
Disobey	Disobeying
	Disobedience
Duly	
E	
Eight	Eighth
	Eighteen
Elegant	Elegantly
	Elegance
Embarrass	Embarrassing
	Embarrassingly
	Embarrassment
Endeavour	Endeavouring
Environment	Environmental
	Environmentally
	Environmentalist

Word	word with different ending(s)
Exaggerate	Exaggeration
Exceed	Exceedingly
Except	Exception
	Exceptionally
Excite	Excitement
	Exciting
Exercise	
Exhibition	
Existence	
Expense	Expensive
Experience	
Extraordinary	Extraordinarily
Extravagant	Extravagantly
	Extravagance
Extreme	Extremely
F	
Fahrenheit	
Familiar	Familiarly
Favourite	
Feasible	
February	
Fiery	
Foreign	Foreigner
Fortune	Fortunate
	Fortunately
Forty	
Fourteen	
Friend	Friendly
	Friendliness
Fulfil	Fulfilment
	Fulfilling
Furniture	
G	
Gallop	Galloping
	Galloped
Gauge	
Govern	Governing
	Government
	Governor

30

Word	word with different ending(s)	Word	word with different ending(s)
Grammar		Intelligent	Intelligence
Grievous			Intelligently
Guarantee	Guaranteeing	Intent	Intention
	Guarantor	Interest	Interesting
Guard	Guarding		Interested
		Irrelevant	
		Irresistible	

H

		J	
Harass	Harassing		
	Harassment	Jealous	Jealously
Heaven	Heavenly	Jewel	Jewels
Height			Jeweller
Heir	Heirloom		Jewellery
Hero	Heroes	Jeopardy	
Hinder	Hindrance		
Humour	Humouring		

K

	Humorous	Keen	
	Humorously	Keep	Keeper
Hungry	Hungrily		Keeping
Hygiene	Hygienic	Key	Keying
	Hygienically		Keyboard
		Kiosk	
		Know	Knowing

I

Identical	Identically		Knowledge
Illegible	Illegibly		Knowledgeable
Immediate	Immediately		
	Immediacy		

L

Imminent	Imminently		
In between		Labour	Labouring
In fact		Laid	
In front		Leisure	Leisurely
Incident	Incidentally	Liaise	Liaison
Independent	Independently	Liaising	
	Independence	Lighten	Lightening
Infinite	Infinity	Like	Likely
	Infinitely		Liking
Innocent	Innocently		Likelihood
	Innocence		
Install	Installing	Likewise	
	Instalment	Literature	
	Installation	Loathe	Loathsome

Commonly Misspelt Words

Word	word with different ending(s)	Word	word with different ending(s)
Lonely	Loneliness	Neighbour	Neighbourly
Lose	Losing		Neighbourhood
Loose	Loosely	Ninth	
	Loosen	No one	
Lovely		Notice	Noticing
Luxury	Luxurious		Noticeable
		Nuisance	

M

Maintain	Maintaining
	Maintenance
Manage	Managing
	Management
	Manageable
Marvel	Marvellous
Mathematics	Mathematician
Meant	
Message	Messaging
	Messenger
Miniature	
Minute	Minutely
Miscellaneous	
Moderate	Moderation
	Moderately
Moment	Momentarily
	Momentary
Month	Monthly
Most	Mostly
Move	Moving
	Movable
Multiple	Multiply

N

Naïve	Naivety
Necessary	Necessarily
Necessitate	
	Necessity
Neglect	Neglectful
	Negligent
	Negligence
Negotiate	Negotiating
	Negotiation

O

Occasion	Occasional
	Occasionally
	Occasioned
Occur	Occurred
	Occurring
	Occurrence
Offer	Offered
	Offering
Old-fashioned	
Omit	Omitting
	Omission
Opportunity	Opportunities
Ordinary	Ordinarily
Original	Originally
Overrule	Overruling

P

Paid	Payment
Paraffin	
Parallel	Paralleled
Paralyse	Paralysing
Parliament	Parliamentary
Particular	Particularly
Permanent	Permanently
Permit	Permitting
	Permissible
Peruse	Perusal
Pigeon	
Poison	Poisoning
	Poisonous
Prejudice	Prejudicial
Prepare	Preparing
	Preparation
Present	Presence
Pretence	
Primitive	

Word	word with different ending(s)
Privilege	
Probable	Probably
	Probability
Procedure	
Proceed	Proceeding
Professor	
Pronounce	Pronouncing
Proof	Prove
Public	Publicly
Punctuate	Punctuation
Pursue	Pursuing

Q

Word	word with different ending(s)
Quarter	Quarterly
	Quartering
Question	Questioning
	Questionnaire
Queue	Queuing
Quiet	Quietly
Quite	

R

Word	word with different ending(s)
Real	Really
	Reality
Receive	Receiving
Recommend	Recommending
	Recommendation
Refer	Referred
	Referring
	Referral
Referee	Reference
Refrigerator	
Religious	
Reminisce	Reminiscence
Repeat	Repeating
	Repetition
Resist	Resistible
	Resistance
Responsible	Responsibility
	Responsibly
Restaurant	
Rhyme	
Rhythm	

Word	word with different ending(s)
Ridicule	Ridiculous
Rogue	
Rough	Roughly
Route	Routing
Routine	Routinely

S

Word	word with different ending(s)
Scene	Scenery
	Scenic
Scissors	
Secret	Secretly
Secretary	
Seize	Seizing
	Seizure
Sentence	
Separate	Separately
Silhouette	
Similar	Similarly
	Similarity
Sincere	Sincerely
	Sincerity
Skill	Skilful
Soldier	
Solicitor	
Souvenir	
Sovereign	Sovereignty
Speak	Speaking
Speech	
Statistics	Statistically
Subtle	Subtly
Success	Successful
	Successfully
Summary	Summarise
	Summarising
Supersede	Superseding
Supervise	Supervising
	Supervisor
	Supervisory
Surprise	Surprising
Survive	Survivor
System	Systematic
	Systematically

Word	word with different ending(s)	Word	word with different ending(s)
T		Vicious	
		Vigour	Vigorous
Tariff			Vigorously
Teach	Teacher	Villain	Villainous
	Teaching	Virtual	Virtually
Technical	Technically		
	Technician	**W**	
Technique		Wednesday	
Temperature		Weird	
Temporary	Temporarily	Whole	Wholly
Tend	Tendency		Wholesome
Terrify	Terrifying	Wield	Wielding
Tomorrow		Wilful	Wilfully
Tongue			Wilfulness
Tragic	Tragically	Withhold	
	Tragedy	Wool	Woollen
True	Truly		
Truth	Truthful	**Y**	
	Truthfully	Yacht	Yachting
Try	Tries	Yield	Yielding
Trying		Yesterday	
Twelfth			
U			
Umbrella			
Undoubtable	Undoubtably		
	Undoubted		
Undue			
Unnecessary	Unnecessarily		
Until			
Unusual	Unusually		
V			
Vary	Various		
	Varying		
Vacuum			
Value	Valuable		
Visible	Visibly		
	Visibility		
Vegetable			
Vengeance			

COMMUNICATION: PART A, PRACTICE TASKS

TASK DESCRIPTION GRID

Number and title	Page	Activities	Refer to reference sheet(s) on page(s)
1 A1 Motors	36	Writing a memo.	6 – 7
2 Telephone Messages	38	Completing telephone message forms.	8
3 Finch and Rook	39	Completing an accident report form. Writing a memo.	6 – 7
4 Ladybird Nursery	40	Writing a memo.	6 – 7
5 The Contented Plaice	41	Taking part in a discussion with a working partner. Designing a poster and including images.	10 – 11
6 Blooming Plants	42	Working with a partner. Designing an advertisement. Writing a business letter.	12 – 13 14 – 16
7 Home Comforts	44	Rewriting a business letter.	14 – 16
8 Home Comforts	46	Writing two business letters.	14 – 16
9 Swan Theatre	49	Writing a business letter.	14 – 16
10 Railway Timetables	51	Researching and writing documents.	
11 Planning a Journey (Derby)	52	Researching and making a telephone call. Writing a personal letter.	17 20
12 Planning a Journey (Lincoln)	53	Researching and writing a personal letter.	18 – 21
13 Pickton Lift Company	54	Researching and writing memos.	6 – 7
14 Hop, Skip and Jump	55	Completing forms, working with a partner to make telephone calls. Completing a telephone message form.	17 8
15 Value for Money	58	Completing a form.	
16 Pets Safe at Home	59	Designing a newspaper advertisement. Writing a business letter.	12 – 13 14 – 16
17 Currently the Best	60	Researching and writing a personal letter.	16, 18 –20
18 Recycling	62	Researching and writing a report. Giving a short talk and taking part in a discussion.	10 – 11, 22 – 26 27 – 28

TASK 1: A1 MOTORS

Student Information

In this task, you will write a memo, using information contained in **Appendices 1** and **2**.

Ask your tutor to provide you with the blank **A1 Motors memo sheet**.

REMEMBER:

A memorandum is a brief, internal written communication.

It can be a formal document (*see page 6* for an example).

It can be an informal document (*see page 7* for an example).

It is signed by the writer.

Writing a memo

Scenario

You work in the Customer Liaison Department of a garage called **A1 Motors**. Today is Friday and you have to inform the Service Department Manager of the number of cars booked in, through your Department, for servicing on Monday to Wednesday of next week.

Activities

Appendix 1 gives details of the cars booked in to the Service Department on Monday to Wednesday inclusive, next week. **Appendix 2** gives details of the registration numbers linked to customers' names.

1   Write the memo from yourself, as the Administration Assistant of the Customer Liaison Department.

     Send it to Ben Trent, Service Department Manager.

2   Use the heading: **Cars booked in for servicing Monday to Wednesday** (dates of next week please).

     You will need to supply the **car registration**, its **make** and **model**, and the **owner's name**. A table might be the best form of displaying this information clearly. Think of the best way of displaying the cars' details on each day of the week.

Appendix 1

Cars booked in . . . .

Monday	X678 TAN (two-day service and repair)
	FR52 OPL
	C48 TOH
Tuesday	SM51 GGR
	NU03 FPQ
	S1 MON
Wednesday	KN02 YKZ
	X231 NOP
	NW51 PLC
	NL03 YSY

Customer Name	Car Make and Model	Vehicle Registration
Pettigrew Charles, Mr	Vauxhall Cavalier	SM51 BVS
Collin Simon, Mr	Fiat Uno	S1 MON
Sturt Adrian, Mr	Vauxhall Vectra	KN02 YKZ
Jenkins Marsha, Mrs	Toyota LandCruiser	NL03 YSY
Clarke Bryan, Mr	Rover 45	NU03 FPQ
Stephenson Craig, Mr	Mini Cooper	SM51 GGR
Stevenson Colin, Mr	Mini Cooper	X231 NOP
Shute Martin, Mr	Range Rover	RR53 RVR
Harton Carol, Miss	BMW 5 series	FR52 OPL
Callisto Henry, Mr	Rover 25	C48 TOH
Jacobs Pauline, Mrs	Renault Clio	X678 TAN
Brentwood Alison, Miss	Rover 75	NW51 PLC

TASK 2: TELEPHONE MESSAGES

Student Information

In this task, you will complete two telephone message sheets.

Ask your tutor to provide you with the blank **telephone message sheets**.

REMEMBER:

Telephone messages are brief.

See page 8 for details of how to take messages.

Telephone messages contain only relevant information.

The information you include must be accurate.

Study the sheets carefully to make sure you complete all the important parts.

Telephone messages

Scenario

You work in a local firm and today take two telephone messages that have to be passed to colleagues.

Activities

1   In handwriting, taking special care of spelling and punctuation, complete the two sheets with the details of the calls. These can be found in **Appendix 1**.

In each case you enter your own name as having taken the message and the time is 10:50.

> **Note**
>
> A completed telephone message sheet contains only relevant information so you need to omit anything which is not necessary to the meaning of the message. Be careful to be accurate in what you write.

Appendix 1

Message 1 – for John Stone, European Director

Daniel Patterson of JK&M Ltd, Denmark, wants to confirm he will be accompanying you on your trip to Lisbon next week.

However, he cannot leave on Monday, as you are doing, because of another appointment which cannot be cancelled. He wants you to know he is leaving on Tuesday on the 08:45 flight from Copenhagen, arriving in Lisbon at 12:20.

If you really want someone from his organisation to be with you on Monday, and he is not sure if you do or not, then he can suggest Erica Lindstrom.

Ring to confirm what you want him to do. He will be out of the office until 4pm our time. You have his number but before 4pm you can reach him by email on dpatterson@jkm.marathon.co.dk.

Message 2 – for Seth Stavely, Sales Manager

Mary Benson of Finch and Rook cannot attend tomorrow's meeting at 10:15. She is sending Peter Farraday in her place. You are requested to give Mary a ring to confirm you agree with the change. Her number is 01904 357 887 (extension 223). She will be in the office until 5pm.

If the call is to be after 6pm then ring her at home on 01904 673 456.

TASK 3: FINCH AND ROOK

Student Information	REMEMBER:
In this task, you will complete an accident report form and write a memo. Ask your tutor for a blank **Finch and Rook Accident report form** and **memo sheet**.	The information you complete must be accurate and relevant. Study the sheet carefully to make sure you complete all the relevant parts. Your memo should be brief and you must sign it. *See pages 6 and 7 on how to write memos.*

Accident report form and writing a memo

Scenario

You work in the offices of **Finch and Rook**, in the Publicity Department and today have to complete an Accident Form to report an accident you saw take place in the restaurant at work.

The accident happened today.

Activities

1   Complete the **accident report form** so that it reflects relevant information shown below:

> ### Accident information
>
> - At 12:10 today you were in the staff restaurant queuing at the counter for food.
> - Michael Winchester was in front of you when he dropped his tray of tea and orange juice on the floor.
> - Next to Michael was Sophia Baxter and as she stepped forward, she slipped on the wet floor.
> - No one had had time to clean the area because immediately after Michael dropped the tray Sophia stepped forward.
> - As Sophia fell her leg twisted under her and she was in obvious pain. She was lying on the floor.
> - The First Aider – Tom Prentice – was called and he suspected a broken ankle and asked for an ambulance to be called. You called for the ambulance and there was a wait of 20 minutes and Sophia was taken to the Wellbeing University Hospital in the town centre at 13:25.
> - She was seen in casualty and diagnosed as having a sprained ankle. Tom was incorrect in his diagnosis of a broken ankle.
> - She was bandaged and sent home at 15:30.

2   Having successfully completed the form, send a **memo** to Andrew Goldton, the Health and Safety Officer, enclosing your form. Use a suitable heading and content in the memo.

> ### Remember
> Your form must be completed neatly and contain accurate and relevant information.
> Correct spelling and punctuation are important too.

TASK 4: LADYBIRD NURSERY

Student Information

In this task, you will write a memo containing information you have extracted from **Appendix 1**.

Ask your tutor for a blank **Ladybird Nursery memo sheet**.

REMEMBER:

Display the information in a way that is easy to interpret.

Make sure the information you give is accurate.

You must sign the memo.

See pages 6 and *7* on how to write memos.

Interpreting graphical information

Scenario

You work in the office of the **Ladybird Nursery**, a children's nursery situated in your town/village . The Coordinator of the nursery is Carol Button and she has asked you to prepare information related to next month's bookings in the nursery.

Activities

1   You are to write a memo to the Nursery Coordinator, Pip Layton.

The purpose of the memo will be to give the Coordinator details of any child who is new to the nursery. This information is needed as it allows staff to better prepare for the arrival of a child new to nursery life.

Extract relevant information from **Appendix 1** to include in your memo.

You will need to provide information on the name of the child, which days and session they will attend, and any other information you consider relevant. To present an ordered and structured document, the names should be in alphabetical order.

Remember to give the memo a suitable subject heading.

Appendix 1

BOOKING RECORD FOR THE MONTH OF *NEXT MONTH*

M am	M pm	T am	T pm	W am	W pm	Th am	Th pm	F am	F pm	Name of Child
✓		✓		✓		✓		✓	✓	Christopher Devlin
	✓		✓		✓		✓		✓	Martha Sutton
		✓	✓			✓	✓	✓		David Squires
✓		✓		✓		✓		✓		**Dene Fletcher**
	✓	✓		✓	✓			✓		**Dene Pollock**
✓		✓		✓		✓				Steven Jefferson
	✓		✓		✓		✓	✓		**Carla Hindmarsh**
✓	✓		✓	✓	✓		✓	✓	✓	**Claire Higginson**
	✓		✓		✓		✓		✓	Katy Fletcher
		✓	✓					✓	✓	Thomas Bentley
				✓	✓	✓	✓			**Louis Trent**
		✓		✓		✓		✓		Gail Breeze
✓		✓		✓		✓			✓	**Anne Forbes**
			✓			✓		✓		Victoria Sykes
	✓	✓			✓				✓	Jamie Westerbook

Shaded rows = new child starting

TASK 5: THE CONTENTED PLAICE

Student Information
In this task, you will work with a partner to plan a poster to advertise a restaurant.

REMEMBER:
Make notes of the discussion you have with your partner.

Use the notes to design a poster.

Design the poster and include relevant image(s).

See pages 10 and 11 on Using Images in Communication.

Ask your tutor if you can have a photocopy of the poster so that you each have a copy.

Working with a partner and designing a poster

Scenario
You are working in a restaurant in Your Town called The Contented Plaice. It serves mainly fish and chips, but has recently begun to offer a variety of snack meals and it is this change that the restaurant wants to advertise.

Today you are to work on an advertisement poster.

Activities

With a partner discuss what will be required to successfully complete the tasks. Then produce the poster together.

Make notes of the things you discuss and keep those notes as evidence. The notes must be organised in such a way that you can transfer topics you have discussed onto your poster.

1   Design an A4 poster (one side only) to advertise the new speciality snacks. Once complete, the poster will go to the local printing company that will print lots of copies for distribution around Your Town.

2   These dishes are:

- jacket potatoes;
- toasted sandwiches with a variety of hot fillings;
- hot dogs; and
- hamburgers.

3   Include relevant images in your poster and any other information you think necessary.

4   The restaurant is open from 11am until 4pm Monday – Friday and 10am to 6pm on Saturdays.

TASK 6: BLOOMING PLANTS

Student Information

In this task, you will work with a partner to design a newspaper advertisement.

Individually write a business letter to the local newspaper asking for the advertisement to be inserted.

Ask your tutor for a blank **Blooming Plants letter heading** and a blank copy of **Appendix 2 Pro Forma**.

REMEMBER:

Make notes of the discussion you have with your partner on the form provided.

Use the notes to design the advertisement (*see pages 12 and 13*).

A business letter is a formal document (*see pages 14 – 16*).

Make sure it contains the following:

- the date it was written;
- the name and address of the recipient;
- a salutation;
- a complimentary close that matches the salutation;
- the name of the person who wrote the letter.

Working with a partner, writing an advertisement and business letter

Scenario

You work for **Blooming Plants**, a garden centre. On the 21st of next month the centre is moving to larger premises. It is your job to deal with two aspects of this move.

Activities

With a partner

Before you can complete this task each of you will have to show you are clear about the objectives of the task and the information you will need to successfully complete the task. For this purpose you will need to complete **Appendix 2 Pro Forma**, which will help with the planning process.

1   Study the information contained in **Appendix 1**.

2   Design a newspaper advertisement to advertise the forthcoming move. It will go in the local paper – *The Bugle*. You should make use of appropriate images.

Your advertisement should be aimed at existing and potential customers.

It should give the date of the move; the last date of trading in its current premises; the opening times in the new premises; the advantages to the customer. Include other appropriate information.

3   To encourage new customers, your firm is going to have a special offer for its first day in the new premises. Decide, together, what that special offer is to be and include details in your advertisement.

Note: You will each need a copy of the advertisement for your individual evidence.

Individually

4   Use the letter heading to write to The Business Advertising Manager, The Bugle, Lord Fullerton's Walk, Your Town YO1 7VQ.4

Ask for the advertisement to be placed in the paper on the 1st, 8th, 10th, 15th and 16th of next month.

For the first three insertions the advertisement should be a quarter-page spread in colour, the remaining insertions you wish to be a colour half-page spread.

Ask for the bill to be sent to the centre's Finance Manager – Bill Cash.

BLOOMING PLANTS

Springbank Lane, Your Town, YO19 5PW

01863- 567 248
blooming@lexodus.co.uk

STAFF NOTICE

As you are aware, with effect from 21st of next month, we will be moving to larger premises and trading from **Vicarage View, Denton, Your Town YO16 4MS**   Our telephone number will be unchanged.

We will cease trading at 7:00pm on 18th and open at 8:30am on the 21st in Vicarage View.

The new location has the advantage of being much larger than our existing site. It is almost three times the size and we have been able to incorporate the following, new, amenities:

- ❀ indoor plant and equipment centre **with specialist staff on duty every hour of opening**

- ❀ outdoor plant and accessories centre **with specialist staff on duty every hour of opening**

- ❀ water garden centre **with specialist staff available throughout opening hours**

- ❀ Japanese garden centre

- ❀ greenhouse centre **with specialist staff to design new greenhouses**

- ❀ garden design centre, open Tuesdays and Saturdays.

New Opening Hours

beginning of April to end of September		**beginning of October to end of March**	
Monday	09:00 – 18:00	Monday to Friday	09:30 – 17:00
Tuesday to Friday	08:30 – 18:30	Saturday	09:00 – 17:30
Saturday	08:30– 19:00	Sunday	10:00 – 14:00
Sunday	10:00 – 15:00		

We are sure the relocation to larger premises will enable us to provide even better services to our existing customers and we hope to attract new customers. Thank you for your co-operation during what will be a busy time.

Holly Bush
Centre Manager

TASK 7: HOME COMFORTS

Student Information

In this task, you will correct a draft business letter that contains spelling errors and is laid out incorrectly.

Ask your tutor for a blank **Home Comforts letter heading**.

REMEMBER:

The letter is known as a **circular letter** because the same letter is being sent to lots of customers.

Make sure it contains the following:

- the date it was written;
- a space where the name and address of the recipient can be added at a later date;
- a salutation;
- a complimentary close that matches the salutation;
- the name of the person who wrote the letter;
- the title of the person who wrote the letter.

See pages 14 – 16 for an example of a business letter.

Writing a business letter

Scenario

You have recently begun working for a soft furnishings company called **Home Comforts** and the Sales Manager, Neil Garner, has handed you a letter he has drafted to his prospective customers.

It is your job today, as his assistant, to ensure a correctly-displayed and correctly-spelt and punctuated letter is ready to leave the firm.

Activities

1   His draft can be seen in **Appendix 1**. You know there are spelling, punctuation and display errors.

2   Prepare a correct version of the letter on the blank letter heading included.

> **Remember:**
>
> Your letter must be laid out correctly and your meaning must be clear.
>
> Correct spelling and punctuation are important too.

HOME COMFORTS

Furnishings of Distinction

119 Mandolin Square   LINCOLN   Lincolnshire   LN1 3BV
Phone:015783644562 **Fax:**015783644652 **email**:HomeCom@Krypton.co.uk

Dear Sir/Madame

I want to take this oportunity to introduce myself and my companie. I have been the Manager of this company since 1987 and my employees and I are all dedicated to providing our customer's with an excellant service to match our top quality goods.

The purpose of this letter is to let you no that for the whole of next month we are offering a outstanding 35% discount of all Grade A carpets and all three-piece suits in the Excelsior range. Furthermore, their will be a 20% discount off all beds and a 10% discount off kitchen ware.

I hope you will visit the store because I am sure you will be delighted with the quality of our goods and the excellence of our service. Alot of our customers return to us year after year and to us, that says our policy of customer care is sucessful.

We all look forward to seeing you next month.

Yours sincerely

Neil Garner   Sales Manager

TASK 8: HOME COMFORTS

Student Information

In this task, you will write two business letters replying to complaints from customers.

Ask your tutor for two blank **Home Comforts letter headings**.

REMEMBER:

Make sure each letter contains the following:
- the date it was written;
- the name and address of the recipient;
- a salutation;
- a complimentary close that matches the salutation;
- the name of the person who wrote the letter;
- the title of the person who wrote the letter.

Include only relevant information and make sure the tone is an appropriate one to pacify a complaining customer.

See pages 14 – 16 for an example of a business letter and page 16 for useful phrases to include in a business letter.

Writing business letters

Scenario

You are the assistant to Peter Burton, the Manager of **Home Comforts Department Store**.

Today Peter has received the attached letters from two disgruntled customers and asked you to reply on his behalf.

Activities

1   Letter from Mr Russon

Apologise. Say you have followed the matter up today and the cheque is in the Accounts Department awaiting the signature of the Head of that Department. You have been assured by him – John Springer – that the cheque will be in tonight's first-class post. If Mr Russon has any queries he should ring Mr Springer on his direct line number – 377 83347.

2   Letter from Mr Cross

Apologise. Say you regret the problem, etc. etc. You have ordered a new sofa in Atlantic Blue today. Manufacturers have been asked to expedite the order and have indicated delivery in three weeks from today. You will contact the customer when the sofa is in the store and arrange delivery.

Offer him the opportunity, once he has a matching suite, of coming in to the store to select up to six cushions that will match his blue suite.

24 Salisbury Avenue
IPSWICH
IP6 4CR

(dated yesterday)

Mr P Burton
The Manager
Home Comforts
119 Mandolin Square
LINCOLN   LN1 3BV

Dear Mr Burton

KITCHEN TABLE

You will recall that ten days ago I returned to your store a kitchen table that was delivered with deep cuts in its surface. This was despite having been inspected by myself in the store and deemed to be in "perfect" condition.

It was agreed over the telephone 7 days ago, that once the table was returned I would receive a refund for the full price - £160.

To date, I have not received this money and wish you to reassure me that I will receive payment within the next five working days.

It hardly needs to be said that I am extremely disappointed, not only in the quality of your products but in your inability to refund money which is due. Should this matter not reach an acceptable conclusion within the time stated, I will have no alternative but to contact the Trading Standards Department of our local Council.

Yours sincerely

Charles Russon

C Russon

"Tulip Cottage"
Milton Green
SUFFOLK
MP3 5BQ

01455   367 3888

(DATED TWO DAYS AGO)

Store Manager
Home Comforts
119 Mandolin Square
LINCOLN
Lincolnshire   LN1 3BV

Dear Sir or Madam

Three-piece suite – Style "Madrid"

I placed an order six weeks ago for a three-piece suite of the above-named style in "Atlantic Blue".

Yesterday the suite was delivered. Unfortunately when my wife and I unpacked it we found that the chairs were of the colour ordered but the sofa is pale brown – called by your delivery men "Fern Brown".

I spoke immediately to the Department Manager – Catherine Welsh – who advised me to write to you to request replacement of the sofa.

Mrs Welsh allowed me to keep the wrongly-coloured sofa as we have nowhere else to sit – two chairs being insufficient for my wife, myself and our three children.

I would be grateful if you would confirm that a replacement sofa will be ordered and delivered urgently. I do not particularly wish to have the unrequired item for any longer than is absolutely necessary.

I look forward to receiving your confirmation that the above request will be actioned.

Yours faithfully

I A M Cross

I A M Cross

TASK 9: SWAN THEATRE

Student Information

In this task, you will read a telephone message from a colleague who dealt with a complaining customer.

You will then write a business letter replying to the complaint.

Ask your tutor for a blank **Swan Theatre letter heading**.

REMEMBER:

Make sure the letter contains the following:

- the date it was written;
- the name and address of the recipient;
- a salutation;
- a complimentary close which matches the salutation;
- the name of the person who wrote the letter;
- the title of the person who wrote the letter;
- the Encs mark after the writer's name and title (to show there is something enclosed with the letter).

Include only relevant information and make sure the tone is an appropriate one to pacify a complaining customer.

See pages 14 – 16 for business letter examples and useful phrases.

Writing a business letter

Scenario

You work in the Customer Liaison Department of the **Swan Theatre, Stratford upon Avon, Warwickshire** and today have to deal with the complaint of a dissatisfied customer. You are replying on behalf of the Theatre Manager, Sunita Patel, so make sure the letter is written as if from her.

Activities

1   Use the letter heading to reply to the complaint which is detailed in the Telephone Message Form below:

TELEPHONE MESSAGE

Taken by: Box Office Manger, Petra Swindles   **Date:** (today)   **Time:** 09:40

From: Cynthia Bumper

To: Theatre Manager, Sunita Patel

Re:

Mrs Bumper arrived at the theatre last night to see "Goodwill in Spring". She had two tickets, purchased by telephone, in Box 7 (Seats 3 and 4).

When she got to her box the seats were already occupied. She reported this to the Duty Manager, Christian Salvason, who allocated her seats in Row T, Numbers 11 and 12.

Mrs Bumper is annoyed, particularly as she purchased the tickets, and received them through the post three weeks ago, and because the seats she and her husband had to sit in were some distance from the stage. They cost £5.00 each, whilst her Box tickets cost £11.00 each.

The Duty Manager assured her a refund would be available if she wrote or telephoned. This she is now doing. She is very unhappy.

Bear in mind the following details for your reply:

- your task is to apologise;
- say that the Duty Manager offered you the seats in Row T because the performance was due to start in only ten minutes and he was anxious to get you seated so you could enjoy the show;
- enclose a cheque for £22 – full refund of the 2 x £11 tickets;
- enclose a £10 voucher which can be redeemed against any matinee performance next month;
- the shows next month, from which she can choose, are as follows:

1st – 7th	Much Ado About Nothing
8th – 15th	The Neighbour's Cat
16th – 18th	Friends for a Day
19th – 25th	Trial by Jury
26th – end of the month	The Boyfriend.

Mrs Bumper's address is:

8 Halfpenny Walk, Stratford upon Avon, Warwickshire WA5 3SF

TASK 10: RAILWAY TIMETABLES

Student Information

In this task, you will locate, and use, a railway timetable in order to find a suitable train.

You will also locate a map of the UK, and mark on it a number of towns.

REMEMBER:

Include your research documents with the task you hand to your tutor.

If you cannot do this, take a photocopy of the documents you find, and attach the copy to the task.

Make sure that all the information you give is accurate and relevant and displayed in an appropriate way so it is easy to understand.

Reading railway timetables and marking places on a map

Scenario

You live in (select a town with a railway station) and it is your Aunt's birthday on the 15th of next month. She lives in (select another town with a railway station about 150 miles away from yours) and your family has decided to treat her to dinner and overnight accommodation on the evening of her birthday.

Locate a railway timetable and map of the UK with which to work on this task.

Activities

1   **Decide upon a train**

It is your intention to meet your Aunt around mid-afternoon, have a look around the shops, and perhaps take afternoon tea, before going to the hotel where she will stay the night and at which the celebration dinner will be held.

Select a suitably-timed train. She would like to be able to make a seat reservation and to have a buffet meal on the train.

2   Decide upon a suitable train on which she can return home the day after her birthday.

She will not want to leave too early as she will probably have a late night with her family the evening before.

Select a suitable train for her return journey, taking into account the previously-stated recommendations about her return home, and her wish to have a reserved seat and, possibly, a meal on board.

3   **Annotating a map**

Obtain a map which shows her home town and yours, and mark on it the place(s) at which the train stops on both its journeys.

TASK 11: PLANNING A JOURNEY TO DERBY

Student Information

In this task, you will locate, and use, a map of the UK, and plan a car journey to a number of towns.

You will locate information about hotels in Derby and select an appropriate one.

You will take part in a telephone conversation to the hotel, with your Tutor acting as hotel booking clerk, in order to make a booking.

Your last task will be to write a personal letter to the hotel, confirming your reservation.

REMEMBER:

Include your research documents with the task you hand to your tutor.

If you cannot do this, take a photocopy of the documents you find, and attach the copy to the task.

Make notes of what you will say on the telephone before you place the call. This will help you to get the conversation right.

See page 17 for guidance on Using the Telephone.

Make notes of what is said to you during the conversation because you will have to use some of this in your personal letter.

A personal letter has your address at the top and the rest of the letter is laid out as a business letter. In this case your personal letter is a formal letter. (*See page 20* for an example.)

Planning a journey by road, booking hotel accommodation by telephone and writing a personal letter to an hotel

Scenario

Next month, you and a friend, who lives in Rotherham, South Yorkshire, are going to spend a few days in Derby. You live in Newcastle upon Tyne. It is fallen to you to arrange the hotel accommodation and plan the car journey from your home, via your friend's and on to Derby.

You must include your source documents.

Activities

1. Using a suitable source – plan the car journey, marking all the major roads upon which you will travel. You will leave your home, drive to Rotherham, pick up your friend and then drive to Derby.

2. Using an appropriate source, find a suitable hotel in Derby.

    You want bed and breakfast for four nights: the first Thursday to Sunday inclusive of next month.

    The accommodation should be close to the city centre and you each have a budget of £50 per night.

3. With your tutor as the Reservations Manager of the hotel of your choice, telephone and make the booking. You will be asked to confirm the booking in writing, and may be asked for other details.

    Make notes because your next task is to confirm the booking.

4. Write to the Reservations Manager, confirm the booking and provide any other information requested in the phone call.

> **Remember you must use appropriate formats for presenting your information, adopting an appropriate style and taking care that your meaning is clear and that spelling, punctuation and grammar are accurate.**

TASK 12: PLANNING A JOURNEY TO LINCOLN

Student Information

In this task, you will locate, and use, a map of the UK, marking towns on the map.

You will locate information about hotels in Manchester and select an appropriate one.

Your last activity will be to write a personal letter to a friend, confirming your forthcoming stay in Manchester.

REMEMBER:

Include your research documents with the task you hand to your tutor.

If you cannot do this, take a photocopy of the documents you find, and attach the copy to the task.

A personal letter has your address at the top and the rest of the letter is laid out as a business letter. (*See pages 218 – 20.*) In this case your personal letter is an informal letter. (*See page 21* for an example.)

Planning journey by road, booking hotel accommodation and writing a personal letter

Scenario

On Friday next week, you and your friend want to travel to Manchester by car. Your friend lives in Lincoln and you plan to drive from your home town of Sheffield to Lincoln to pick him/her up, then drive to Manchester and stay in a city centre hotel for three nights, before reversing the journey.

Activities

1   In order to have some idea of which parts of the country you will be visiting, mark Manchester, Lincoln and your home town of Sheffield on the map.

You will, of course, need to consult a reliable reference source in order to do this task accurately.

2   Use a UK Hotel Guide to find a suitable hotel in Manchester in which you can stay for bed and breakfast. You wish to be in the city centre and each has a budget of £60 per night.

Make a note of the name, address and telephone number and details of any facilities it offers, e.g. swimming pool, leisure complex, etc.

3   Write a personal letter to your friend.

Advise him/her of the hotel you have chosen and tell him/her the day and date you will collect him/her from their home.

Add any other information you consider relevant.

TASK 13: PICKTON LIFT COMPANY

Student Information

In this task, you will locate, and use, temperature details about two cities abroad.

You will use the information you find to write two memos to members of staff.

Ask your tutor for two blank **Pickton Lift Company Memo sheets**.

REMEMBER:

Include your research documents with the task you hand to your tutor.

If you cannot do this, take a photocopy of the documents you find, and attach the copy to the task.

You can make your memo formal (using the recipient's full name and title), or informal (using just their name). Be consistent in how you use your name/title.

Remember to sign the memo.

See pages 6 and 7 on how to write memos.

Conducting research and writing memos

Scenario

You work for **Pickton Lift Company** and the company exports its lifts all over the world.

Some staff are going on a sales trip in the last week of next month and it is your job today to find out the weather and temperature in each area being visited.

The staff and destinations are as follows:

Geoffrey Clarke, Sales Manager   Rio de Janeiro, Brazil

Amanda Gregory, Sales Director   Lisbon, Portugal.

Activities

1   Using appropriate reference sources and websites, find and print out the required details for each place being visited.

2   Write a memo to each member of staff attaching the print out/copy of source document relevant to them.

The memo must be headed: Your forthcoming visit to .... (put in place name). Word the memo appropriately.

You are writing the memo and your position is Office Assistant, Travel Department.

> #### Remember:
>
> Your source documents should be included with your task.
>
> Your memo must be laid out correctly and your meaning must be clear.
>
> Correct spelling and punctuation are important too.

TASK 14: HOP, SKIP AND JUMP

Student Information

In this task, you will use information contained in **Appendix 1** and **2**, to complete expense forms for three employees.

You will also make two telephone calls with a partner then complete a **Telephone Message Sheet**.

Ask your tutor for three blank **Hop, Skip and Jump Expense Forms** and a **Telephone Message Sheet**.

REMEMBER:

Be accurate with the information, and calculations, you include on each form.

Complete the forms neatly.

Make notes, before your telephone calls, of what you will say.

See page 17 for guidance on Using the Telephone.

Make notes of what is said during the telephone calls because you will use this information to complete the Telephone Message Sheet.

See page 8 for details of how to take messages.

Use only relevant information on the telephone message form and be sure to be accurate.

Completing expense forms, working with a partner and making telephone calls then completing a telephone message form

Scenario

You work as a Finance Clerk in the Finance Department of a company called **Hop, Skip and Jump**, a company that manufactures shoes based in Your Town.

Today you are to complete several tasks to do with employees' expense forms and hotel bookings. Details of the Approved Hotel rates can be found on *page 56*.

Activities

Working alone

1   **Appendix 1** gives you details of the expenses being claimed for three members of staff as a result of recent business trips.

      Complete an expense form for each person.

      You can sign as having passed each form for payment.

      Note: Staff can only stay in the **Approved Hotel** in each destination. You have a list to refer to when entering details of overnight accommodation.

Working with a partner

2   Your company has now won a major contract in Ipswich and you have to ring **two** hotels – **The River View Hotel** and **The Star Inn** – to find out the rates they charge.

      You will need to place **two** telephone calls so you can both take the part of the Hop, Skip and Jump employee, and the hotel employee. One of you will ring The River View Hotel, the other will ring The Star Inn. Prior to making the calls you will need to make notes about what you are going to say in both your roles. Read **Appendix 2** carefully first because it contains some instructions.

Working alone

3   Having got the information you need from the calls, you must complete the telephone message sheet, giving Robert Bouncer, the Finance Officer, the information.

HOP, SKIP AND JUMP

APPROVED HOTELS

HOTEL ACCOMMODATION DETAILS
(Approved hotels and expenses per person per night)

Town/City	Name of Hotel	Cost per person per night £
Chichester	The Star and Garter	76.00
Croydon	The Golden Cross	66.00
Edinburgh	McMurray Hotel	56.80
Exeter	The Westerner	75.35
Huddersfield	Yorkshire Dragoon	45.75
Lincoln	Master and Hounds	62.95
London	Fullingham Lodge Hotel	117.50
Morpeth	The Borderman	53.85
Portsmouth	The Pheasant Inn	73.80
Rotherham	Carlton Hotel	54.75
St Albans	The Coach Inn	84.00
Swindon	The Goddard Arms	94.00
Taunton	Atlantic View	67.45
Wilmslow	The Mancunian	88.50
York	The George and Dragon	75.00

Appendix 1

Expense claim details for last month

Purchasing Division

Matthew Joyce

5th Office to London by train	£107.00	Overnight in London Hotel
19th Office to Lincoln by car	£64.90	Overnight in Lincoln Hotel

Aaron Clifford

19th	Office to Taunton by train	£166.00	Overnight 19, 20 and 21st
22nd	Taunton to London by train	£93.60	Overnight in London
13th	London to office by train	£134.00	No accommodation

Marketing Division

Beverley Grant

4th	Office to Chichester by train	£107.00	Overnight in hotel
5th	Chichester to Office by train	£107.0	
8th	Office to Morpeth by car	£113.55	Overnight in hotel
9th	Morpeth to home by car	£113.55	

Telephone Call Instructions and Guidance

Hop, Skip and Jump Employee	Hotel Employee
You will need to give the name of your company and **possibly** an address and your name and position.	You will need to identify your hotel and ask for the name of a person to whom you are talking.
Your company anticipates making bookings for around six nights a month – bed and breakfast – one employee staying on each occasion for one or two nights.	You will wish to have an estimate of how many bookings per month will be involved.
You wonder if there are special "company" rates?	You quote a price of around £57 per night (**there must be at least £10 difference in the cost the two hotels' prices**).
Make it clear staff will pay their own bill upon checkout, i.e. you do not want the bill sent to the company for later payment.	Before you can quote an exact rate, you would need to have a request in writing from Hop, Skip and Jump.
You want to know the **latest** check-in time.	The latest check-in time is 18:30 unless the hotel receives a telephone call on the day of arrival advising of a later time.
You wonder how many days notice the hotel will require of a booking, i.e. three days, five days ten days, etc.	The hotel would need to have any booking requested no fewer than three days before arrival.
As your company has been asked to put something in writing, get the address and post code of the hotel.	

This is the information you must give or find out. How you do this, the sequence you use and what other information you feel appropriate is up to you.

Do not make each telephone call identical!

TASK 15: VALUE FOR MONEY

Student Information	REMEMBER:
In this task, you will complete a **Customer Complaint and Refund Form**. Ask your tutor for a blank **Value for Money Customer Complaint and Refund Form**.	Be accurate with the information you add to the form. Sign the form yourself and get a colleague to sign it as the customer.

Completing a customer refund form

Scenario

You work in the Customer Services Department of **Value For Money Supermarket**. A customer has come to the desk with a complaint concerning being wrongly charged yesterday for tomatoes.

Activities

1   Complete the **Customer Complaint and Refund Form** with the relevant information from the information below.

> Mr Leonel da Silva, yesterday, purchased 2 kilos of Spanish tomatoes priced at 85p a kilo.
>
> His receipt shows he was charged for Cherry tomatoes at a cost of £1.60 per kilo.
>
> The store has decided to refund twice the difference in cost and issue a discount voucher valued at £2. This voucher can be redeemed against any goods in the store in the next 30 days.
>
> Mr da Silva lives at 6 Jackson Street, Your Town BN3 3MX.

Sign the form yourself as the Staff Member, and get a colleague to sign as Mr da Silva.

Use appropriate dates.

TASK 16: PETS SAFE AT HOME

Student Information

In this task, you will design a newspaper advertisement.

Complete an advertising coupon with the wording of your advertisement. Ask your tutor for a copy of the **Advertisement Coupon**.

Write a business letter to a local newspaper asking for the advertisement to be inserted. Ask your tutor for a blank **Pets Safe at Home Letter Heading**.

REMEMBER:

Be brief but accurate with the information you put in the advertising grid.

Write a formal business letter and decide upon a suitable heading for the letter.

You should include an **enc** to indicate something is being enclosed with the letter.

See pages 12 and 13 for advice on writing advertisements.

See pages 14 and 15 for an example of a business letter and page 16 for useful phrases to include in a business letter.

Designing a newspaper advertisement and writing a business letter

Scenario

You are the Assistant to Bertie Bassett, the Advertisement Manager in the Publicity Department of **Pets Safe at Home** based in Your City.

Your firm offers a "pet sitting" scheme for holiday makers and, as such, has a register of staff upon whom it can call, relating to their particular interest or special knowledge.

The local paper – *The Gazette* – is running a promotional offer with all advertisements at half price for five nights.

Your job today is to design the advertisement and write the letter of confirmation to the Business Advertisement Manager.

Activities

1   Design the advertisement. Remember your aim is to attract custom, so the wording is important. Although the advertisement will be half price, it will be charged per insertion, and your company does not have money to waste.

   Complete the Advertisement Coupon (ask your tutor for a copy).

   You want prospective customers to realise that you will look, not only after their pet(s), but their home during their period of absence. An additional service is the care and maintenance of greenhouses and indoor/outdoor plants, together with essential food shopping immediately prior to the owner's return.

2   Write to the Business Advertisement Manager at the newspaper and arrange to take up the special £15 single insertion offer, for Monday to Friday nights next week (i.e. five insertions).

> **Note**
>
> This special offer allows for a maximum of 25 words at a charge of £45, before charging another 5p for every word over that amount. (A telephone number counts as one word.) The advertisement size is a quarter-page boxed spread.
>
> **You are not required to calculate the cost, merely to remember WORDS COST MONEY!**

TASK 17: CURRENTLY THE BEST

Student Information

In this task, you will conduct some research into consumer law.

You will then write a personal letter to a store, quoting relevant sections of your researched documents.

REMEMBER:

Include your research documents with the task you hand to your tutor.

If you cannot do this, take a photocopy of the documents you find, and attach the copy to the task.

Write a formal personal letter, including accurate details.

Use a suitable heading for the letter.

See pages 18 – 20 for an example how to set out a personal letter.

See page 16 for some useful phrases.

Your tone should be appropriate to the task – polite, but firm.

Conducting research and writing a personal letter

Scenario

A number of weeks ago you bought a new Portiflex iron from your local electrical shop.

You discovered the iron was faulty – described as "steam 'n' spray" and did neither!

You returned the iron to the shop but were told by the shop assistant that it was not their problem and you must write to the manufacturer.

Dissatisfied with this you wrote to the Manager of the store and received the reply **shown in Appendix 1**.

Having spoken to a friend, you are vaguely aware that your rights as a consumer are not being taken seriously and decide to do some research then reply to Mr Simonds.

Activities

1. Find relevant information to help you write to the Manager. You should look for information on Consumer Law in the UK, particularly related to the Sale of Goods Act and the Trade Descriptions Act.

   Provide copies of your source documents

2. Use the information you obtain to reply to Mr Simonds saying that you will be returning to his store next Saturday and expect to receive a full refund. Make it clear you are not obliged to accept a Credit Note, nor are you willing to accept one on this occasion. You need also to mention it is not your responsibility to contact the manufacturer as your contract is with the store as the seller of the faulty goods.

   For each statement you make you must support it with facts.

   > **Note**
   >
   > You will be expected to select an appropriate style and tone and to make your meaning clear, using accurate spelling, punctuation and grammar.

CURRENTLY–THE–BEST
ELECTRICAL STORE

Unit 15, Tilbury Retail Park, Your Town, SK6 3BC
Tel: 01347 4776 2228

(Dated 2 days ago)

Mr/Ms
63 Sunnyville Court
Your Town
SK11 8JS

Dear Mr/Ms

Portiflex Iron Model Spray'n'Steam SuperLuxe

I thank you for your recent letter concerning the purchase of this model of iron for the sum of £35.99. Unfortunately, as my assistant told you when you came into the store, I am unable to help in this matter.

The iron you purchased was sent to us by *Portiflex* and was deemed to be in satisfactory condition and good working order at the time we took delivery of it. As the iron was boxed when you bought it from us it is a matter for the manufacturer to deal with your complaint. I am sure if you return the item to them (address as follows), you will receive a satisfactory outcome to your complaint.

Portiflex (UK) Ltd, 11 Empora Way, Your Town, CH8 15SR

I apologise for this but trust you will realise the matter is out of our hands. You must deal with the manufacturer. Certainly we cannot refund your £35.99, nor can we exchange the iron.

However, as a mark of our goodwill, we are prepared to take the iron back and issue you with a credit note for the sum you paid for the iron. You will have to spend this money in our store within 21 days.

I look forward to hearing from you and wish you success with your complaint to *Portiflex* should you decide upon that course of action.

Yours sincerely

R Simonds

R Simonds
Store Manager

TASK 18: RECYCLING

Student Information

In this task, you will locate, and use, information on **recycling**.

From this research you will prepare:

a) a report;

b) information for a short talk.

You will produce a document to hand to the audience which will contain at least one appropriate image.

REMEMBER:

Include your research documents with the task you hand to your tutor.

If you cannot do this, take a photocopy of the documents you find, and attach the copy to the task.

Make sure that all the information in your talk is accurate.

The image(s) you use will be appropriate and enhance the audience's understanding of the topic.

See pages 10 and 11 for help on using images in communication.

See pages 22 – 26 for help on writing reports.

See pages 27 and 28 for help on giving a talk.

Conducting research and giving a short talk

Scenario

You work in a **The Contented Plaice** fish restaurant, on a part-time basis, and have been concerned, for some time, that it throws away vast quantities of glass and newspaper each day. You mention this to your boss, Margaret Aislaby, and she is impressed by your enthusiasm for, and concern about, the environment. She asks you to put together a report and some information in order to give a short talk to herself and the restaurant's staff.

Activities

1. Conduct some research into the topic of recycling, using the Internet if possible, **and** paper-based sources and write your report.

    You will need to include copies of your source documents and **at least one of these must contain an appropriate image that you will use and explain in your talk.**

    You may wish to consider the following recycling issues:

    ● what can be recycled by your restaurant;

    ● methods of recycling;

    ● the advantages of recycling;

    ● facts/figures concerning recycling.

2. Give a short talk about your findings, ensuring you include a document with at least one image, which you will hand to the audience. The talk must last no fewer than four minutes and no longer than six minutes.

> ### Note
> Be prepared to answer questions from the audience following your talk.

SAMPLE END ASSESSMENT

20 Multiple-choice questions

The following questions are multiple-choice. There is only one correct answer to each question.

Instructions

1 Choose whether you think the answer is A, B, C or D.

2 Ask your tutor for a copy of the answer grid (or download a copy from **www.lexden-publishing.co.uk/keyskills**).

3 Enter your answer on the marking grid at the end of the test.

4 Hand it to your tutor for marking.

A Communication Key Skills Level 2 External Assessment will consist of 40 questions and you will have **1 hour** to complete them.

How will you select your answers?

If you are sitting your End Assessment in paper format – not doing an online test – you will have to select one lettered answer for each numbered question. The answer sheet will be set in a similar way to the example below:

1   [a] [b] [c] [d]

2   [a] [b] [c] [d]

Make your choice by putting a **horizontal line** through the letter you think corresponds with the correct answer.

Use a pencil so you can alter your answer if you wish and take an eraser to allow you to change your mind about a response. Use an **HB pencil**, which is easier to erase. (If you make two responses for any one question, the question will be electronically marked as **incorrect**.)

Take a **black pen** into the exam room because you will have to sign the answer sheet.

Your tutor has 100 sample End Assessment questions and you will be given these when your tutor considers you are ready to practise the questions.

QUESTIONS

In December 1954, there occurred in London one of the fiercest tornadoes recorded in Britain. A thunderstorm rushed in from the South Coast. The sky turned black an a tornado smashed trees near Hampton Court.	Line 1
Around 5pm the storm reached Chiswick, West London, and there were reports of a huge conical cloud hanging down from the sky, green lightning flashing from its sides and a deafening roar. The tornado hit two factories and tore Gunnersbury station apart.	Line 5
Other damage incurred that day included roofs ripped off houses, chimneys crashing down and walls collapsing.	
A car was reported hurled through the air and windows were rattled violently. The only protection for the terrified people caught outside was to run for cover to try to avoid the barrage of bricks, glass and wood which were thrown through the air.	Line 10
When all was calm and the tornado had passed, news programmes showed a scene of devastation that was described as looking like something from the Blitz.	Line 15
Winds in the tornado's vortex reached an estimated 160kph (100mph) and left a trail of devastation for several miles, finally petering out around Golders Green and Southgate in North London. Remarkably, there were few casualties.	Line 20

Questions 1– 5 refer to the text above.

1 The style of writing in the article is **best** described as:

A informative

B persuasive

C entertaining

D technical

2 Which of these words could **best** replace the word **"conical"** as it is used in **Line 5**?

A round

B square

C tapering

D balloon-shaped

3 In the fifth paragraph, which word would best replace the words **"When all was calm and the tornado had passed"** without altering the meaning of the sentence?

A Furthermore

B Later

C Formerly

D Remarkably

4 Which of these words could best replace the word **"barrage"** as it is used in **Line 11**?

A path

B onslaught

C whirlwind

D number

5 According to the article, which of the following statements is true?

A London was well-prepared for the storm.

B Very little damage was done but the tornado was unexpected.

C There was a lot of damage and some people were killed.

D There was a lot of damage but few people were injured.

	33 Swanley Drive Lincoln Lincolnshire LN1 3BY

13 March 2007

Mr J Lines
Customer Services Manager
North Yorkshire Moors Railway
Grosmont
North Yorkshire
NY15 7NP

Dear Sir

Last week, on Tuesday, I <u>traveled</u> on the train leaving Pickering at 10:20, expecting to arrive in Grosmont at 12:25.	Line 1
When I boarded the train and entered a carriage I found it was strewn with litter and the windows were dirty on the inside, so much so that it made it difficult to see what was advertised as "beautiful scenery". When the train arrived at Levisham it was <u>unfortunatley</u> delayed and I did not arrive in Grosmont until 13:05. I, and several other <u>passenger's</u>, tried to establish from railway officials on the train, the cause of the delay, but our questions were not answered.	Line 5
<u>Alot</u> of the passengers were annoyed at the delay and I was unhappy about the attitude of the Station Master at Grosmont when I complained.	
I am extremely disappointed that these events and attitudes made what should have been a pleasant day into an unpleasant one and I wish you to look into the matter and let me have your comments in the next seven days.	Line 10
Yours sincerely	
Colin Crown	Line 15

Questions 6 – 11 refer to the letter above.

6 The Salutation should have read:

   A   Dear Mr Crown

   B   Dear Mr Lines

   C   Dear Sir or Madam

   D   Dear Customer Services Manager

7 The <u>underlined</u> word on **Line 1** should be spelt:

   A   travveled

   B   travelled

   C   travled

   D   travelld

8 The <u>underlined</u> word on **Line 5** should be spelt:

   A   unnfortunately

   B   unfortanatly

   C   unfortunately

   D   unfortantly

9 The <u>underlined</u> word on **Line 8** should be spelt:

   A   Allot

   B   A lott

   C   All lot

   D   A lot

10 The <u>underlined</u> word on **Line 6** should be spelt and punctuated:

   A   passengers

   B   passengers'

   C   pasengers

   D   passengerr's

11 The writer has chosen to start a new paragraph on **Line 10** because he:

   A   wants to emphasise how much he is annoyed

   B   is describing what he wants done

   C   wants to complain about the whole day

   D   is summarising his feelings and detailing what he wants to occur next

To	Carol Trent	From	Jane Swift	
	Sales Manager		Personnel Manager	
Date	11/10/2007			Line 1
Re	Sunday Trading			

In reply to your recent <u>query</u> concerning the hours which are <u>permitted</u> for Sunday Trading, I can give you the following information. In this country if retail premises open on Sunday, the maximum trading hours are six. Therefore, we could open at 10am and close at 4pm, or alternatively, 11am until 5pm. We must not exceed these permitted hours. I trust this information is helpful. If you wish to discuss this further, please telephone me.

Line 5

Questions 12 – 15 refer to the text above.

12 This document is an example of:

A   A telephone message

B   A letter

C   A memorandum

D   A report

13 An alternative for the first word underlined on **Line 3** would be:

A   question

B   suggestion

C   assistance

D   problem

14 An alternative for the second word underlined on **Line 3** would be:

A   insisted upon

B   obligatory

C   encouraged

D   allowed

15 The date should have been written as:

A   11 October

B   11 October '07

C   11 October 2007

D   11/10/2007

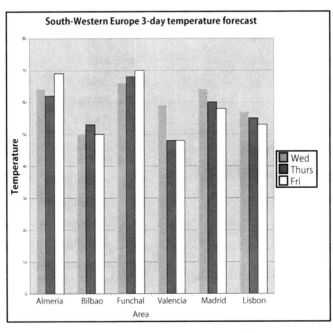

16 On the chart, which **Area** has the highest temperature on Wednesday?

A   Lisbon

B   Almeria

C   Funchal

D   Madrid

Outward journey

From	To	Date	Dept/Arrive	Journey time
Bristol Temple Meads	Exeter Central	Fri 17/12/04	10:14 11:24	1h 10m
Bristol Temple Meads	Exeter Central	Fri 17/12/04	10:40 11:50	1h 10m
Bristol Temple Meads	Exeter Central	Fri 17/12/04	11.16 12:16	1h 00m
Bristol Temple Meads	Exeter Central	Fri 17/12/04	11:20 12:40	1h 10m
Bristol Temple Meads	Exeter Central	Fri 17/12/04	11:44 12:44	1h 00m
Bristol Temple Meads	Exeter Central	Fri 17/12/04	12:16 13:38	1h 22m
Bristol Temple Meads	Exeter Central	Fri 17/12/04	12:44 13:54	1h 10m
Bristol Temple Meads	Exeter Central	Fri 17/12/04	13:44 14:54	1h 10m

Return journey

From	To	Date	Dept/Arrive	Journey time
Exeter Central	Bristol Temple Meads	Fri 17/12/04	13:50 14:00	1h 00m
Exeter Central	Bristol Temple Meads	Fri 17/12/04	14:00 15:33	1h 33m
Exeter Central	Bristol Temple Meads	Fri 17/12/04	14:46 16:19	1h 33m
Exeter Central	Bristol Temple Meads	Fri 17/12/04	15:00 16:33	1h 33m
Exeter Central	Bristol Temple Meads	Fri 17/12/04	15:10 16:43	1h 33m
Exeter Central	Bristol Temple Meads	Fri 17/12/04	15:19 16:25	1h 06m
Exeter Central	Bristol Temple Meads	Fri 17/12/04	15:45 17:25	1h 40m

Questions 17 and 18 relate to the railway timetable above.

You want to travel to an interview from your home in Bristol to the interview in Exeter on Friday 17 December. Study the timetable and answer the following questions:

17 Your interview starts at 12:30, and you will have a 20-minute walk from Exeter Central station. Which train would you be advised to catch from Bristol Temple Meads?

    A   the 10:14

    B   the 10:40

    C   the 11:16

    D   the 11:20

18 You assume your interview will be over by 13:35 and you want to get back to Bristol as quickly as possible. If the interview **does** end at 13:35, which train would be the **first** you would be likely to be able to catch?

    A   that arriving at 16:19

    B   that arriving at 14:00

    C   that arriving at 15:33

    D   that arriving at 16:43

Questions 19 and 20 relate to apostrophes.

19 Which sentence is correct?

    A   The men's hats' were left on the bus.

    B   The mens' hat's were left on the bus.

    C   The men's hats were left on the bus.

    D   The mens' hats were left on the bus.

20   A   The children's presentation is sheduled for next month. Do you think you'll be able to present the prize to the sucessful child?

    B   The childrens' presentation is scheduled for next month. Do you think you'll be able to present the prize to the successful child?

    C   The children's presentation is scheduled for next month. Do you think you'll be able to present the prize to the successful child?

    D   The childrens presentation is scheduled for next month. Do you think you'll be able to present the prize to the successful child?

INDEX

INTRODUCTION	**1–3**
Application of Number	1
Communication	1
Improving Own Learning and Performance	1
Information and Communication Technology	1
Log Book	3
Mandatory Key Skills	2
Portfolio Front Sheet	3
Portfolio of evidence	3
Problem Solving	1
Wider Key Skills	2
Working with Others	1

COMMUNICATION	**5–28**
Advertisements	12–13
column	13
designing	13
display	12
line	12
lineage	12
Commonly misspelt words	29–32
Forms	
message	9
Images	10–11
Letters	18–21
business	14–16
key to parts of	16
personal	18–19
to a company	19–20
Memos (memorandum, memoranda)	6–7
Messages	8–9
form	9
identifying the key facts	8
Numerical data, presenting	
in graphs	10
in tables	10
Presentations	27–28
closing	28
delivering	27
images	28

openers	28
preparing for	27
questions	28
reading	28
Reports	22–26
bibliography	24, 25, 26
conclusions	24, 25
content	25
context	22
findings	24, 25
main sections	24
objective	22
parts of	23
recommendations	24, 25
source material	22
structuring	23
terms of reference	23, 25
title	25
title page	24
Talk, giving a – *See Presentations*	
Telephones	17
answering	17
placing a call	17
speaking on	17

Lightning Source UK Ltd.
Milton Keynes UK
01 June 2010